GOOD GRIEF

Also by Theresa Caputo

There's More to Life Than This

You Can't Make This Stuff Up

GOOD GRIEF

HEAL YOUR SOUL,
HONOR YOUR LOVED ONES,
and LEARN TO LIVE AGAIN

the
LONG ISLAND MEDIUM

THERESA
CAPUTO

with
Kristina Grish

ATRIA BOOKS

New York   London   Toronto   Sydney   New Delhi

ATRIA BOOKS

An Imprint of Simon & Schuster, Inc.
1230 Avenue of the Americas
New York, NY 10020

First Atria Books hardcover edition March 2017

ATRIA BOOKS and colophon are trademarks of Simon & Schuster, Inc.

For information about special discounts for bulk purchases, please contact Simon & Schuster Special Sales at 1-866-506-1949 or business@simonandschuster.com.

The Simon & Schuster Speakers Bureau can bring authors to your live event. For more information or to book an event, contact the Simon & Schuster Speakers Bureau at 1-866-248-3049 or visit our website at www.simonspeakers.com.

Interior design by Amy Trombat

Manufactured in the United States of America

10 9 8 7 6 5 4 3 2 1

Library of Congress Cataloging-in-Publication Data is available.

ISBN 978-1-5011-3908-6
ISBN 978-1-5011-3910-9 (ebook)

For my family, friends, and everyone on Team Caputo whose support, love, and generosity fill me with so much gratitude, I could burst! Thank you for respecting my gift and helping me spread Spirit's messages.

For God and Spirit, who never allow for a dull moment and always have our healing in mind.

Contents

Looking Up

Welcome to Good Grief

If you've picked up this book, it's pretty safe to assume that a loved one has passed or that you'd like to support a friend or family member going through the grief process. So I want to first say that I'm so sorry for your loss, and feel so grateful that you trust me to hold your hand during this challenging journey. And while I realize you're suffering, I also need you to know there *is* hope and healing in your future. It is not a coincidence that you have my book in your hands. Something made you stop and believe that *this* time, in *this* book, you'll read what it takes to finally fill the aching hole in your heart. Listen, that "something" you felt wasn't a coincidence or gas from the chicken curry you ate for lunch. It was your loved one's soul, their ever-present energy, speaking through yours. It's their greatest hope that you learn to heal and carry on.

Where did I get this intel? Well, as you may know from watching my reality show *Long Island Medium*, reading my books, or catching a shockingly accurate spoof about me on *Saturday Night Live* or *Jimmy Kimmel Live!*, I'm a medium. This means I sense and feel Spirit that's around us every day—a.k.a. the souls that love, protect, and guide us from Heaven, including God, angels, spirit guides, souls of faith like saints, and departed loved ones. I've been on a one-on-one basis with Spirit since the age of four, though I didn't hone my abilities until I was in my late twenties (as an uber-Catholic, let's just say it took a while for me to accept my abilities). Once I felt confident that talking to souls who walk in God's light is, in fact, a gift from Him, I devoted myself to helping people work through their sorrow by channeling their loved ones' healing guidance. What's amazing is that I've found it always gives them the reassurance, comfort, and kick in the pants they need to truly mend their souls. Heaven knows none of this comes from *my* brain—I'm as surprised as anyone when I say what I do! I am simply a vessel for messages that come from a Creator who knows a lot more about how the universe works than you or I possibly could.

Sharing Is Caring

What I *have* always known is that someday I'd put the best of Spirit's healing advice and client stories into one book, and Spirit recently showed me that the time is now. Across cultures, we've become increasingly open about our feelings and instincts, not to mention curious about the Other Side. Whether I'm at the store or manicurist, or just minding my own beeswax at the deli, there's a good chance I'll meet strangers whose loved ones passed, and they'll pour their hearts out to me. Sometimes the person does it hoping Spirit will come through, but this happens to friends who don't talk to dead people too. The truth is, when you lose a person you love, the feeling is so raw that it consumes you. Immediately, you find a way to edge it into any conversation, as if you couldn't possibly talk another minute without telling your story—never mind if it's relevant or if the listener wants to hear any more about it. Am I right?

While I'm sure there's a psychological term for this behavior, Spirit says it's all good. Sharing your pain shouldn't feel awkward or forced— in fact, it should feel as natural as sharing joy. Sharing, in general, has a spiritual purpose because we learn from and lean on each other as a community. We form connections that on some level remind us that we also share a universal consciousness—in other words, that we're all in this together. It's important that we learn the tools that can help us to help each other out.

At the end of the day, Spirit says that when you're faced with a loss, you have a choice about how you grieve. You may feel defenseless at first, but you are responsible for how you manage grief because you have been given innate tools to navigate it. God has instilled in us both instinct and free will, and just as we use them to meet our soul mates or pursue our passions, we must also use these tools to champion heartache and honor loving memories. Try not, then, to feel powerless to grief because choice can give you the control you crave. For example, you can choose to keep your feelings to yourself or express them, to visit a cemetery alone or celebrate your loved one with a party. You can decide how to carry on their legacy and what you'll believe about the afterlife. You can opt to welcome their signs and symbols and invite their souls to guide you every day. Plain and simple, *you* make the call on whether you'll live the rest of your years with joy and peace, or with fear, guilt, anger, and sadness. Life goes on either way.

How to Use This Book

I want to talk about the tone of this book, which may seem unusual for one about grief! At times, Spirit's guidance will swing from tough love to compassion to ridiculous optimism, and I need you to go with me on this. When I channel souls, this is how they approach the healing process—in a frank but mostly warm and positive way. To Spirit's mind, death has ended their lives but shouldn't end yours. Your ability to cope with grief is seen as a challenge that will make you stronger, wiser, and more capable than before. It will teach you lessons that grow your soul. It will help you grasp how important love is, to move ahead with positivity, and to appreciate those around you. So I don't want you to ever think I'm being flip or insensitive, or underestimating your pain based on how I present Spirit's POV, because that's not the case. And while Spirit's words are sometimes hard for me to say, I deliver them with faith and ask that you hear them with faith too. Spirit tells us what we need, not what we want—and it's all blessed by God.

Good Grief's chapters are written to be read in order, with the hope that they will echo your grief process, but by no means is that necessary. Because everyone grieves differently, and our emotions bounce around like a wild kid in a bouncy castle, feel free to jump to a chapter that feels more in tune with what you're experiencing at the time—if, and only if, you promise to eventually read what you skipped. Spirit wants you to absorb the entire book because even if a chapter topic doesn't seem to hit home at one point, it will at another. There are thirty-one chapters total, so pace yourself. You might even want to work on this over the course of a year, averaging a chapter every week and a half or so—but again, your timeline is up to you. Spirit just asks that you don't complete the book in one sitting. We want you to consume, savor, and digest it until you're good and full.

Finally, you'll find exercises at the end of each chapter, and though it may be tempting to ignore them, please don't. They are integral to Spirit's plan for you. Some of the ideas came from your loved ones' souls, others are from my angels and guides, and the rest are from clients who've truly found their way. Don't worry, there won't be a test at the end! But my divine sources say that you will feel a calm mind and peaceful soul, which is, like, a million times better.

Now take a deep breath, thank your loved one for guiding you here, and let's get started.

GOOD GRIEF

1

Learning from the Best

You know that famous book All I Really Need to Know I Learned in Kindergarten? It's about simple yet life-changing advice that the author remembers from his childhood, like "don't hit people," "share everything," and of course, "flush." I mention the book here because its premise reminds me of how I've come to deliver simple yet life-changing messages to my clients—except all *I* really need to know I learned from channeling God and your loved ones' souls! They're the most amazing teachers and have taught me so much about grief that can help you embrace life after a loved one passes.

I feel it's important to credit God and Spirit right off the bat, because it helps explain why I say and recommend what I do. I'm not a therapist or bereavement counselor, and there's probably some etiquette about handling grief that I've never been taught. As a medium, however, my duty is to tell you what Spirit feels will help you carry on without your late aunt, child, or spouse, and this can be very different from what a trained grief counselor might suggest. For example, Spirit needs you to know there's more to life than what's here in the physical world, and that your loved ones are still with you, just in a different way. Now, that's not something most books about grief would drive home, fair enough? Yet this and other guiding principles from Spirit are what truly help my clients repair and rebuild their lives.

And while Spirit and I have helped bring hundreds of thousands of clients peace during their grief process, I don't have a ton of heavy, *personal* experience with this topic in my own life. It's kind of crazy— the first time I lost a close loved one was when my Nanny Brigandi passed away; I was sixteen years old at the time, and then seven years later, her husband, my Pop, died. It was really hard to lose my father's parents. But after that, life gave me a major sabbatical from grief. For almost *twenty years* I didn't experience a death-related heartache again. What *did* happen, however, was that I accepted and honed my ability to communicate with all kinds of souls in Heaven, including God, angels, spirit guides, and your departed loved ones who've taught me everything I know. In other words, I learned about healing through the universe's lens, not my own. I was never distracted by my own drama and was forced to stay focused on Spirit's messages. Having nearly two decades of constant, objective, spiritual training was part of God's plan for me—and clearly for you too.

Getting the Gist of Grief

Since the beginning of my career, I've channeled a theme that runs throughout all of Spirit's messages: "You will grieve your loss for the rest of your life, but healing is something different." What Spirit means here is that you must find ways for your grief and healing to coexist, because no matter how a person dies, you will always have to live without someone you love and that sucks. I think one of the scariest things about death is that it introduces you to ugly emotions you've never felt before—devastation, jealousy, fear, betrayal, abandonment—and they hit you like a ton of bricks. To experience a death that's so close to you might even force you to confront your own mortality for the first time. Grief is especially hard because it's not every day that a situation demands you walk the line between feeling your heaviest feelings so you can heal and trying to protect yourself from getting stuck in a negative place. So instead of doing what's best from the start—processing the loss, honoring your loved one, and carrying on in a positive way—you may end up on a dark and twisted path even when you crave light, direction, and calm.

What I love about Spirit's guidance is that their goal is to help heal your soul. From there, they say, everything else will fall into place. For soulful healing to occur, you must realize that your loved ones give you permission to feel the pain, but also ask that you learn and grow from it. They explain that God and your loved ones want you to be happy. As you begin to internalize this, you see the importance of loving yourself and others, functioning with a positive outlook, and staying busy at a pace that feels good. This makes it easier to appreciate the signs your loved ones send and value the rapport you still share, since you trust that the soul bond is never broken. Having an ongoing relationship with the departed then makes it easier to value the living. You increasingly feel supported by souls on this plane and on the Other Side as you figure out your new normal. Grief gradually begins to define less of your day, because while death can be a painful reality for the living, you realize that your loved ones are at peace and their passing was never meant to stop your journey outright. You shed anger and practice forgiveness, and eventually you are able to appreciate the universe's big picture: that everyone's soul is created from God's perfect love, and our purpose is to use that love to enrich your life and that of others.

At first, healing is about surviving heartache; in time, it's about feeling joy despite it.

Listen, I'm not saying that any of this is easy. In fact, Spirit says healing from grief is one of the hardest obstacles we face on earth, but it's important work that we must all do in this lifetime. Try as you might, nobody escapes this lesson—grief transcends cultures, social classes, education, genetics, and more—because navigating grief is essential to maturing every one of our souls. We gain new understanding, acceptance, compassion, and a better ability to communicate with the Other Side when we grieve. We are here on earth to learn and grow, and unfortunately grief is a means to that end. It is a rite of passage for the soul.

Practicing What I Preach

A few years ago, I was finally able to apply Spirit's teachings to my own grief process. I should have known Spirit wouldn't let me off the hook for too long! While my maternal grandmother, Gram, was the first person to pass after my little grief hiatus, it was actually her husband's death that had the potential to emotionally wreck me if I hadn't taken Spirit's advice into consideration.

When my mom called to tell me that my grandfather, who we called Gramps, wasn't doing well, I rushed to the hospital for a visit. I was in the middle of taping my TLC show *Long Island Medium*, and even in four-inch heels, I got there pretty fast! Right away, I felt Gram's soul in the room and knew she was there to help him cross over. I said to Gramps, "It's OK to go with Gram now." He was weak and lethargic that day, but managed to shake his head no. Gramps was always stubborn, so I don't know why I thought his passing might be any different! And though the next day Gramps was strong as an ox—sitting up, eating well—his burst of energy didn't last. The following morning Gramps died. I did not get to say a final good-bye to my grandfather, who passed from complications from end-stage renal disease.

Now, somebody else in my sparkly shoes might have felt haunted by Gramps's death—maybe upset about not visiting when he was at his best or regretful about not being with him when he died—but because I'd learned about grief for all those years, I was better able to cope. For one, I knew that our loved ones never want us to feel any burdens, guilt, or regrets around their passing. So instead of getting upset that I didn't get to see Gramps full of piss and vinegar, I thanked God that our final visit was as good as it could be that day. And while I wasn't with him when he passed, I also remembered that if Spirit says you're not in the room at the time of a death, that soul did not want to leave you with the burden of seeing its body take its last breath. I believe this is the case with Gramps.

I've also followed Spirit's advice in how I celebrate and remember Gramps to this day. I try to stay positive for the rest of the family, since this is what Gramps would have wanted, and regularly honor his memory. I'm quick to talk about how playful yet ornery Gramps could be, and every time I order his favorite split pea soup at the local luncheonette, I think of him and know his soul is with me as I do. When I miss Gramps, I remind myself that Spirit says, "The only thing that's been broken is our physical connection. Our soul bond will never end," and I know from channeling Spirit that I will see Gramps again when he greets my soul in Heaven. Until then, Gramps wants me to live in a way that makes me feel happy and spreads positivity to others. I grieve Gramps every day, but doing this under Spirit's wing has helped me acknowledge his passing and feel appreciative of all we shared during this lifetime.

I'm not meant to be the only one who absorbs and practices Spirit's healing lessons! God and your loved ones want this for you too. And while Spirit says our destiny is set, our freewill choices are what fill in the details of our lives. How you recover from loss is one such decision, and it impacts the strength of your eternal soul. Look, I know it's broken into a million pieces right now. But it would be an honor and a privilege if you allowed me and Spirit to help you put it back together. What do you say?

Healing Moments

Even if you don't change out of your plaid pajamas, you're going shopping today. I'd like you to buy a journal that you'll use to work through some of your feelings, thoughts, and memories as we move through this book together. You will also use this space to complete guided exercises—and honestly, write about any other experiences you have during your grief process too. So find one you really love—red leather, leopard print, a composition book, it's up to you! I want you to enjoy how this journal looks and feels, because it will be one of your most cherished companions as you heal.

2

So Now What?

When it comes to a loved one's passing, Spirit often makes me feel that death itself is the "easy part." Not easy-easy, like gaining-ten-pounds-over-the-holidays easy, but simpler than the grief process you have to face in the weeks, months, and years to come.

Shortly after a person dies, there's always something to do, someone to take care of you, and ways to honor that loved one's memory. You might not even realize it at the time, because you're busy making phone calls and funeral arrangements, and spending most waking moments with family and friends. You sort through old photos and belongings, and tell stories about the person you loved. You laugh, cry, both, neither—it doesn't matter, because there are no expectations around what you should feel or do. Everything and nothing is normal because you're encouraged to grieve in whatever way you need. It feels as if other people's sympathy, generosity, presence, and homemade crumb cakes will never end.

But the pace, company, and understanding do slow down. And man, does it get quiet.

The Cheese Stands Alone

After the initial flurry that comes with laying your loved one to rest, it's normal to feel like your life has come to a complete halt while everyone else's moves on. You have been forever altered, yet the world doesn't change its plans or pace on your account. People have babies, buy houses, go on vacation, become grandparents—and here you are, left to pick up the pieces alone. Despair and isolation dominate your thoughts. You don't know how to talk about your feelings, yet you feel disconnected from anyone who tries to ask. You wonder if this is bad behavior, but you're secretly too exhausted to care. You don't recognize your life or any of the relationships in it. You feel utterly alone, confused, and lost at sea.

This reminds me of how my client Clara felt after she lost her husband, Jo, to a heart attack while they were on a cruise. For two weeks after the funeral, her home was full of food, friends, and family. "You can't imagine the trays of breakfast meals, sandwiches, pasta, meatballs, eggplant," she says. "We ate and talked about Jo, and everyone took turns helping out with the yard work. It was really insane, the generosity of people." Yet after three months, Clara felt a jarring shift. "Friends and family went back to their familiar lives, whereas mine became drastically foreign and lonely," she said. "My finances and parenting prospects had changed. I came home to an empty house every night." Adding insult to injury, life also became logistically harder. "I started walking to and from the bus station, because I had nobody to drive me," Clara said, "and when it rained, my dad had to drive a half hour to pick me up."

When clients feel this kind of initial sadness and displacement, Spirit acknowledges it and then assures them that sparks of hope *are* within reach. To demonstrate this in a reading, loved ones bring up happy memories that make you smile, but you can just as easily recall them on your own. Spirit's intention isn't to rub your nose in the past but to show you that if you can respond to a story in a positive way, you are capable of feeling temporary breaks in sadness—if not genuine, occasional joy. The more you allow yourself to feel and experience good things, the more room you'll make for other encouraging thoughts to carry you along. Look, I'm not saying you'll feel the *same kind* of happiness you did before your loss, but the emotional and practical upheaval that comes with death will feel a little more bearable.

And for now, that's something, right?

You Just Call Out My Name . . . and You Know, Wherever I Am . . .

During this initial period, Spirit also needs you to believe that while you can't see or touch your loved ones anymore, their souls never leave you. You may feel like your relationship is over, but you actually have a new kind of relationship with your loved one, thanks to an ongoing bond that will never end. It isn't a physical relationship anymore, but a spiritual and soul bond relationship that lasts forever. I can't tell you how often Spirit says to me, "Yes, I died. But I'm still the same. I'm just in a different form."

Clients always think the souls of the deceased are waiting for them at the graveyard, floating above them on a cloud somewhere, or that I bring them to a reading (um, no thank you)—but none of this is true! Heaven isn't that far away, and your loved ones are with *you* anytime you call on them. Souls communicate through thought, so when you want to talk to your deceased loved ones, you don't have to put on a show to get their attention. You don't even need to speak out loud. You can silently communicate to Spirit with your thoughts and the feelings you project, and they'll hear you. In fact, it's your loved ones' job in the afterlife to watch over, guide, and protect those they love on earth. True, Spirit can't drive you to the bus station or pick you up in crummy weather, but as guardians, they *can* help you get a cab if you ask or if you talk to the soul in your mind, keep you company while waiting for your ride. And please, don't be deterred from interacting with Spirit just because you can't see them. A lot of us have a solid relationship with God, and you can't see Him! Faith plus instinct is what offers proof.

Your loved ones are also around during activities that make you feel close to them. This is one of the reasons Spirit asks you to keep up traditions and routines like baking holiday biscotti or sleeping in their concert tees—their souls are present when you do something that remembers, honors, or simply includes them. I once read the cutest elderly man who lost his wife, and her soul said, "He's all about his routine, Theresa. Every morning, he still makes us oatmeal and pours us both a cup of coffee!" The man laughed sheepishly. "I still do that, it's true," he told me. "I talk to her like she's still with me"—and the wife's soul responded, "I hear every word. I *am* still with him, please tell him that."

Milestones are just as important to Spirit. I can't tell you how many souls say they attend weddings, graduations, births, reunions, vacations, and other meaningful events. On these days, Spirit says to look out for signs—birds, pennies, feathers, license plates, songs, or anything odd or weird that reminds you of your loved one. This is how souls say hello from Heaven. I'll get into signs and symbols later, but for now, know that your loved ones use their energy to direct your attention toward the object—Grandpa's soul isn't in the robin, and your late aunt is not a feather. Souls can do this faster and with more ease when you're less distracted by your own sorrow and open to spiritual moments going on around you.

So why do souls even bother to come around? Why don't they just cross over and do, you know, soul things? I'm shown they stick close for two reasons. First, God's unconditional love bonds all of humanity and exists in every person's soul. This love forms energetic connections between us. Your relationship can even become stronger when your loved ones' are in Heaven because they're with you all the time, whereas you might have seen your cousin Jenny only four times a year when she was alive! Second, your soul is bonded to loved ones through what I call a "soul circle"—a group of souls, including your closest friends and family, that reincarnate together in every life. As a member of a soul circle, you play different roles in loved ones' lives—your husband might be your brother in your next life, and your sister in this life might have been your mom in a prior one. I talk more about soul circles in my other books, but I want to briefly mention them here because it's consoling to know that when the soul of a loved one passes, your relationship keeps going. You remain connected on this plane, see each other when you transition, and reincarnate together in future lifetimes. Your bond is eternal. Being aware of a grander scope here is helpful, as it shows that everything has a purpose and is working for a greater good.

Healing Moments

Whip out that new journal! For your first entry, I'd like you to write down one happy or positive memory about a loved one that happened before the person passed away. Maybe it's about how you went for brunch every Sunday or that time you talked until midnight over a ridiculous amount of hot cocoa. You can write one sentence or fill an entire page, but the more specifically you remember these special times, the more cathartic it will be. Souls can sense your feelings and musings, so know that your loved one is with you as you do this activity. "You will not forget me," Spirit often says. "And when you think of me, I am with you." Let a week pass, and then go back and reread what you wrote. How does it feel to remember the past this way? Did you feel any relief by putting it on paper? Why do you think that is?

3

Grief, Healing, and
Your New Normal

As you might guess, Spirit says most of us don't understand what it means to grieve and heal, which is one reason it's so hard to do. This isn't your fault—socially, we have very few role models to help set our expectations about what happens to us when a loved one dies. And while grief and healing go together like salt and pepper or ketchup and mustard, they are very different things. To truly heal your life and soul, it helps to understand Spirit's take on these two concepts and their relationship to each other.

Grief and Healing: Birds of a Feather

Grief is a natural, normal response to loss, and though you will grieve your loved ones for the rest of your life, how you demonstrate that grief is unpredictable and changes as time goes on. Initially you might uncontrollably sob and visit the cemetery every day. Or you might cry only on holidays, hold off on purchasing a headstone, and feel closest to your loved one when you're alone in the garden. You might never cry at all, but you might punch pillows. Maybe you'll realize you don't like to share your feelings, or you'll talk about them nonstop and then worry you've said too much. Listen, all of this is OK! Who's to say what's acceptable? Spirit says grief responses are like snowflakes—no two are the same. The way water molecules arrange themselves in a snow crystal is almost infinite, and there seem to be unlimited expressions of heartache too. All of them are valid because they capture your feelings at that moment.

While there are no clear-cut emotions to feel or activities to do to find peace, Spirit says that situations and relationships—both within and outside your control—will influence how you move through your grief process. They cause the intensity of your sadness to swing, progress, and regress. Spirit says you are not getting better or worse as these variations occur, but simply experiencing the fluctuations of grief. This is why Spirit says grief doesn't always sequentially arrive in those famous five stages—denial, anger, bargaining, depression, and acceptance—but skips around with variations on each theme. You might feel denial or anger for a few months, then a short period of depression, then a resurgence of anger, and then unexpected calm. You're grieving the whole time, just in different ways.

Even so, the most complicated grief process must include the intention to embrace life again, which is what Spirit considers healing. Healing does not mean forgetting what happened or what life used to be like. It means that your days, no matter how weird or horrible they feel, go on and so must you. Spirit wants you to experience your grief without letting it hold you back from living in the here and now.

Spirit's suggested grief process, then, incorporates healing techniques that help you put one foot in front of the other. These might include reminiscing about your memories, accepting help and support, releasing burdens and guilt, and taking care of yourself and those around you. Just as grief unfolds differently for everyone, so does the healing that your soul requires. For some, it makes the greatest impact to talk to a counselor about your struggles and how to adjust to life without your loved one. Others might hold on to anger, reach a turning point when they let go of negative baggage related to the death, and then suddenly feel whole again. No matter who you are or what your story is, Spirit says that healing is essential because it returns you to a functional mind-set, and spiritually it grows your soul and that of the person who died. Healing is hard work, but every effort results in a more mature perspective. It's from this place of wisdom and strength that you can then enrich your time here and shape those around you.

Spirit says this is a good time to remind you that while it feels like your world's gone mad, you have so many reasons to carry on. Your loved ones are happy. They are at peace. They are safe with God. Their souls visit you all the time. They're with those who died before them, participating in activities they love, learning lessons, and exploring other dimensions. In fact, they urge you to heal so that *you* will feel safe, happy, peaceful, and grateful for your current life too. They want you to laugh, enjoy the rest of your time here, and not feel so alone. They want you to respect and love yourself again, and move on to a more positive mind-set as you keep plugging along, learn lessons, and fulfill your purpose in this world. As you know, one of Spirit's jobs is to guide you, and by healing your soul, you're actually making their job a little easier! They can focus on helping you along your soul's path instead of helping you recover from their passing. They can usher you toward the fulfillment you deserve and that God wants for you too.

"I Just Want to Feel Normal Again"

The most common refrain I hear from clients is that they want everything to go back to feeling the way it did before their loved ones died. "I just want to feel normal again," they say. But that's just crazy—how are you supposed to feel normal after someone you love dies? It's not possible. And then if clients *do* start to feel a little better—not amazing but maybe with longer stretches between days spent in a haze—they worry that they're not remembering or honoring their loved one enough since they're carrying on! It's as if constant grief makes them feel closer to the soul and heavy emotions become confused with love.

When it comes to healing, life as you once knew it is not what you're after. Spirit says the goal of grieving and healing is to find a *new normal* that you can accept. You won't go on the same, but you will go on. You will never be "the old you," but that doesn't have to be a bad thing. It's a different thing, a different you, and maybe someday it will be a way to live with more wisdom, compassion, and courage.

Finding a new normal is not a smooth or easy discovery, as a mother named Cindy reminded me, but it is possible—even after the most horrific traumas. Cindy's son Nicholas took his own life at twenty-one years old. He'd been in a car accident the year before and suffered a severe brain injury that went undiagnosed. He began experiencing symptoms similar to ADHD, so he saw a psychiatrist who prescribed medicine for him without actually testing for the disorder. As a result, Nicholas stopped eating and sleeping, and experienced mood swings and heart palpitations. His mom begged her son to stop his meds, so the doctor gave him a different one. Three weeks later, while babysitting his younger siblings with his girlfriend, she left the room and Nicholas strangled himself. Cindy was certain that her son's misdiagnosis and treatment changed his health, personality, and judgment, though the police and autopsy reports treated his death like a routine suicide. Sure enough, when I channeled Nicholas at a live show in Charlotte, North Carolina, one of the first things he said to me was "Tell my mom it was the medicine."

When Cindy's son first died, her grief hit her like a ton of bricks. "My immediate feeling was shock," she said. "When the ER doctor told us he was gone, all I could do was vomit." Cindy then crawled onto the gurney with Nicholas; she kissed him and told him she loved and forgave him. The next few days were a blur, and Cindy stayed in bed for weeks. She dreamed that she saw Nicholas in a crowd or that he was lost and she'd have to find him. When Cindy woke up each morning, she'd be reminded all over again that her son was gone, and she would weep. "It was about six months before I could wake up and not cry," she told me. Nicholas's death also traumatized his siblings, who were nine, eleven, and sixteen years old when he passed. His youngest brother almost immediately exhibited serious signs of anxiety, depression, and PTSD; her daughters were also affected, but in different ways.

Even so, for the sake of her sanity and children, Cindy found it in herself to adjust her perspective on what her family's life had become. "I knew I would never be the same and that my life was forever changed. I knew I would never be 'me' again," Cindy said. "But my children had their whole lives ahead of them, and I'd be damned if I'd let this ruin them. I told my kids we would find a 'new normal.' "

After five long years, Cindy's family has done everything they can to accept their new reality. The kids are homeschooled and try to live in a way that honors their brother. To celebrate Nicholas's memory, Cindy had a street named after him on his high school grounds and stays in touch with his friends. She believes her son's soul hasn't left her and can hear her when she speaks to him. She tries to focus on what's really important, knowing that nothing is guaranteed and that you have to give life your all. "I have made the effort to maintain my friendships instead of holing up in my room," she said. "I loved music and lost it for a while, but I enjoy it again. I can appreciate beauty in nature again too. I am so proud of my children for how hard they have tried to get better. Life now differs from life before, but our goal is to live the best life we can after this tragedy. To get up every day and live, really live." Cindy listened to her soul and takes one day at a time. She is doing her very best within reason and reality, and that's all Spirit asks of you too.

Healing Moments

Set aside five minutes when you can sit quietly in a chair with your feet on the ground, or on the floor with your legs in a yogi pose (a.k.a. lotus position). Imagine yourself in a bubble of God's pristine white light. Close your eyes, and then take three deep breaths in and three out. Do this until you are breathing steadily and feel increasingly relaxed. In this peaceful state, I want you to think about just one way to adjust your life toward an acceptable, new normal. It can be a small effort—maybe right now, folding your laundry, going to an outdoor concert on a pretty afternoon, or seeing a friend for lunch would feel like progress. Visualize yourself doing these things and asking for help if you need it. Imagine how it feels to accomplish these tasks. You can end here or try integrating one of the positive changes into your day. Spirit will be by your side either way.

4

Grieve from Your Soul

While another person's death was not your choice, Spirit says you must use your free will to elect how you will grieve and whether you will heal. I realize that after feeling like your heart's been torn from your chest and put through a paper shredder, asking you to find the initiative and inner strength to come back from this is a tall order. It's extremely hard for me to say it too, but Spirit always insists I do. They have tremendous compassion for what you're going through, but their top priority is to help you keep going.

The reason for Spirit's concern is simple. Grief has the power to transform who you are, what you value, and how you see the world. There's no way grief won't alter you to some extent, so Spirit says you have to be mindful about how this happens and the degree to which it impacts the rest of your life—and on a deeper level, your core being. The most honest and pure way to grieve, then, is from your soul. This ensures that every feeling and instinct that influences your choices comes from a divinely inspired source.

Feel Your Way

Your genuine feelings are stored in your soul, as is your intuition, so when you honor and act on your feelings, two things happen. First, you grieve from the most genuine part of you, and second, your instincts steer the type of healing you need as you need it. Just keep in mind that as you make choices based on how you feel, you must also take active steps to heal. So if you *feel* like you need to stay in bed, that's what you should do, but promise yourself that you'll get out of the house tomorrow. Or if you *feel* like seeing a friend, meet her for a cup of coffee and then use that time to help yourself feel better, whether that's talking about what's on your mind or hanging out in a way that makes you feel loved. Your feelings may even encourage you to do somewhat uncomfortable tasks like forgive a loved one by writing his soul a letter or letting go of pent-up anger by screaming like crazy at the stars. No matter how you specifically feel your way through grief, trust that your soul would never steer you wrong. God gave us our intuition to use when maneuvering through life, and it excels at challenges and traumas.

Your instincts are like a built-in GPS system that lives in your soul, which makes it your greatest tool in life, and especially as you grieve. Using your intuition to navigate grief reminds me of how I used it to bring up my kids, because that was a very instinctual process for me. Though I had a billion opinions at my fingertips, how I chose to raise Little Larry and Victoria was really up to me. I might have listened to a friend's advice about nutrition, an in-law's take on sleep training, and paged through some magazine tips on how to soothe a temper tantrum—but I ultimately did what *I* felt was right. It doesn't mean these other well-intentioned sources weren't valid or helpful, they just didn't all work for me. In the same way, a friend or counselor might suggest perspectives, advice, or theories about how to carry on, but only you know what sounds and feels best. Picking and choosing from other people's ideas, then checking in with yourself about each, is a nice way to make sure you are grieving in tune with your soul.

If you're on the fence about trusting your own judgment during such a harrowing and unstable time, I'm gonna let you in on a little Spirit-fact that might make it easier for you to have faith in your gut. The reason our instincts usually come through for us is because a lot of our gut-urges come from Spirit. God, angels, spirit guides, and other spiritual beings including your loved ones nudge the small, quiet voice in your soul that suggests important choices that feed your happiness. And as you grieve, Spirit tells me that *a lot* of these inklings come from your loved ones because they're so invested in your healing. Listening to how your soul tells you to move through grief, then, is a really nice way to partner with your loved one to heal. It also reinforces your relationship with that soul and reminds you that it is ongoing.

Grieving from your gut isn't just about doing what feels good; it's about paying attention to seemingly odd or unique instinctual cues—like a sudden urge to sort through your departed father's old ties or hum your deceased cousin's favorite jazz tune. There's a good chance that this is what your soul needs and that the inspiration comes from a loved one's energy. This reminds me of a client who was having dinner with his mom when he suddenly remembered a touching story about his deceased dad. He wanted to blurt it out, but decided to stay quiet because he was afraid of bumming out his mom, who was having a great time. Though the boy had thoughtful intentions when he ignored his hunch, during a reading with me, the father's soul said he wished his son had shared the memory because it would have been very healing to the family. Dad also said his soul prompted the story in the first place! Though Dad's soul was still with his family during their meal, they missed out on the opportunity to feel the healing energy that comes when we honor those we love. The family might have even missed out on a comforting sign. Because Spirit can hear and feel your words, thoughts, and emotions, they like to show us they're around by doing cool things like giving us chills, flickering the lights, or directing our attention to signs. It's their way of being part of the action!

Most important, when you allow your soul to guide your healing, try not to doubt what you feel and know that Spirit's guidance will always be positive. Loved ones and other well-intentioned Spirit *never* encourage you to have thoughts or feelings tinged by doubt, fear, or negativity. Spirit is all about helping you find a happy ending.

Take Your Time

Grieving from the soul means honoring your own unique timeline for healing. It is not God's plan for you to become stuck in your grief indefinitely, but there is also no typical response to loss. One year, three years, a decade—who cares? Grief is a process. Healing faster does not mean healing better. Nobody has the right to tell you when to "get over it" and how to behave during this period, because only *you* know the meaning of what you shared and how your soul feels after loved ones pass. If your brother dies, you and your sister-in-law may have lost the same person, but each of you has unique and special memories that define your relationships and will inform how long you mourn. Your loss, and so the time it takes to heal, is extremely personal.

It's easy to compare the length and severity of your grief to that of others—like an acquaintance in your support group, or a friend who also loved the person you lost—but Spirit says to stop wondering if you should be doing something more or different and focus on *doing what's right for you*. This reminds me of when Gramps died, and although my whole family of course grieved, it was my aunt Gina who seemed the most devastated because she grieved at a much "slower pace" than the rest of us. It would be so easy for an outsider to assume that Gina was stuck in her grief or held on to her sorrow longer for some subconscious, deliberate reason. But Spirit says she simply listened to what her soul needed, which was more time to feel her way through a traumatic loss and come out the other side as best she could.

Over two years passed before Aunt Gina felt herself slowly beginning to heal. For her, this meant crying a little less, being able to casually talk about Gramps, and having a genuinely good time at family gatherings. "I never asked people to feel sorry for me," she said. "I just wanted to be left alone to grieve my way, for as long as I needed. Grief is a process, and I had to follow my instincts." I knew Aunt Gina was making progress when she turned a video of Gramps—decked out in his submarine hat and jacket, telling war stories—into a DVD for all of her sisters. "Even though my dad is no longer here, I can finally listen to his stories and laugh," she said. Being able to share these memories was a sign that she was ready to open up a little more about who Gramps was to her and invite others to celebrate him the same way.

Healing Moments

Take a cue from Aunt Gina's DVD about Gramps by turning one of your fondest memories into a treat for others. Go buy your Nana's favorite breakfast cookies from the bakery she loved, then give half to your neighbor or make a mix of your uncle's top twenty tunes for his favorite nurse at the assisted living center where he lived. When you hand over the present, be sure to tell the positive story behind it, and take a moment to feel your loved one's energy in the room as you talk about what he or she meant to you.

5

Life's a Real Beach

Grief is often compared to larger-than-life natural forces like mountains, avalanches, and even tsunamis. I've also heard that it resembles a roller coaster because grief causes you to feel fast-changing emotions. These are all fair correlations, but Spirit says grief is most like a wave on the beach of life. Think about it: Grief ebbs and flows. You may feel a wave of grief coming on, but it can also blindside you. If you're not careful, a wave can suck you in. It's like your sorrow is controlled by a force so much bigger than you, and so far out of reach that it might as well be the moon. And though your grief feels all-powerful now, eventually the water will recede and the waves won't rise as high. Still, you must learn how to swim.

When Triggers Make Waves

Because grief waxes and wanes, but never really leaves you, most counselors warn against what they call "triggers"—anything that brings up memories related to a loss—that wreak havoc on your emotions. Triggers might seem obvious and easy to predict or completely catch you off guard. What's interesting is that while it's normal to respond to triggers negatively, Spirit needs you to know that some are misunderstood, others are set up by your loved ones, and all are an opportunity to recognize that your loved one is with you at the exact moment that the trigger happens. Is that an amazing twist or what? Realizing and accepting this news from Spirit can really help calm the ripples of grief that you feel.

Special days like birthdays, holidays, or anniversaries are said to be triggers, but Spirit actually prefers that they're used as an opportunity to happily honor and remember your loved one. Whether you release a balloon, grab a slice of pie at their favorite diner, drive past their old home, or plant a sunflower in their memory, such moments invite Spirit to spend time with you. The truth is, it's typically the day *after* a predictable calendar date that needs a little planning. I have an acquaintance who, on the fifth anniversary of her brother's death, was fine because a lot of people called or wrote tributes to him on Facebook—"all in all, not a terrible time," she told me. But the next day? "I could barely leave the couch," she said. "I called in sick and cried all day. I haven't done that in a while, but my body and heart needed a time-out." Imagine if she'd anticipated this response and made plans with a friend for lunch or a run in the park instead? She still would have felt the impact of her loss but maybe her entire day wouldn't have gone south. At the very least, she'd have ridden out her afternoon on a raft of support and love.

Whether you're planning to honor your loved one on trigger days or mitigate your sadness after, Spirit insists that you don't put a lot of pressure on making their soul the focus of the *whole* day. When you attach enormous expectations to a plan this way, you run the risk of not seeing it through and then feeling that you let yourself or your loved one down. One simple activity is *more* than enough. Think about the things your loved one liked to eat, do for fun, do for others—that kind of thing. I remember reading a client who lost her mom, and the soul kept showing me a pocketbook and the department store Kohl's. She said, "Tell my daughter to grab her bag and the coupons—we're going shopping!" As it turned out, the daughter said she'd hit the sales to honor her mom, coupons in hand. She'd even announce, "Come on, Mom, we're going to Kohl's!" You can do the same or make a whole list of stuff your loved one enjoyed, and if you have the energy after doing one to keep going, do another! And while you miss your loved ones most on these days, Spirit says they don't miss us the same way because they're always *with* us! It's hardest on the living because we have to continue on without seeing them physically.

Finally, everyday triggers can invite waves of grief, but Spirit says not to let them pull you under. The real meaning behind these otherwise harmless moments gets lost in translation when you're too caught up in your pain to see it. So when banal activities open the floodgates—say, when walking the dog or cleaning out the car makes you feel wistful— Spirit says not to feel their absence too heavily. You are typically having this flood of emotion because a loved one's energy is actually nearby and on some level, your body and soul can sense it. Say hello and talk to the souls in your midst the next time this happens.

A member of my fan club named Shannon said that connecting with her late mother's soul when she encounters a trigger has really helped her healing process. When Shannon first lost her mom to a rapidly progressing cancer, she said, "I cried at some point every day—gut-wrenching, desperate tears. That grief was like a freight train." During this period, she felt a deep sense of loss when she had automatic thoughts like "I should call Mom" and realized she no longer could, or saw a car like her mom's and expected it to be her. But in time, Shannon came to see that these triggers were actually validations that her mom's energy was alive and well. Now, for example, when she's anywhere near Costco, she thinks of her mom and smiles rather than cries, since Mom was an avid bargain hunter. Shannon also swears that she can hear Mom's advice in her head when she cooks. "When adding ingredients, I can feel Mom saying, '*Whoa, whoa,* ENOUGH!' or when adding flour to my homemade pastry,

'Paaatience, paaatience, take your time. . . .' " Rather than allow these moments to produce overwhelming grief, Shannon embraces them as proof that her mom's soul is aware and part of her life.

Fears Create Swells Too

To me, the most threatening waves of grief are fed by unfamiliar fears and animosity that you can't always control or ignore, no matter how hard you try. These responses seem to come out of nowhere, making you feel even more uncomfortable. This might include wondering if you're cursed, getting annoyed at people you once felt close to, or worrying about things you'd never thought twice about before. I was reminded of these kinds of fear-based responses when I channeled the soul of a thirteen-year-old boy named Dustin at a show in Fargo, North Dakota. While riding his dirt bike home from seeing his best friend, Dustin was hit by a car that broke his neck on impact. "Dustin's death is the far worst thing I've ever felt," his mom, Laurie, said. "I don't think I will ever 'get over it.' The best I can do is keep going."

As for so many of my clients, surprising post-traumatic waves of fear and paralysis are very real for Laurie and her daughter Katie. "Katie is scared to death that something will happen to me and she'll grow up alone, so she tries to please others, is very sensitive, and cries a lot. She also doesn't sleep well, and as a second grader, says other kids don't understand her." As for Laurie, she says she's "paranoid now and will check things many times—did I shut off the oven? Lock the doors?—even if it means having to drive home ten miles. I used to leave lights on, but now I won't even do that. I shake when the phone rings."

When I channeled Dustin, his soul went to the heart of his family's worries so that he could help alleviate potential damage to his mother's and sister's souls. He said he's so proud of his sister and that he knows she's very scared of her mom getting hurt or dying, but that he is watching over and protecting them. Laurie says this has helped Katie tremendously, especially when she's away from her mom at school. He encouraged Laurie to take back her life, so she tries to live in a way that would make Dustin proud. She's become closer to his biological dad, and in fact, the three attended a holiday "Parade of Lights" and sponsored a float in Dustin's honor that said "We believe in angels." Laurie talks about Dustin daily and feels more compelled than ever to help others like he did, since he passed after helping his best friend fix his bike. And while at one time Laurie wasn't sure she'd ever leave the house again, after her reading she took a part-time job at a nursing home and volunteers at a funeral home. She and Katie look for signs from Dustin and pray to him every night for guidance. Laurie and Katie know that while grief is stronger some days than others, Dustin's presence is constant.

The thing is, you don't need a private reading with a medium to learn that Spirit wants you to find ways to navigate around your post-traumatic fears when they keep you from embracing life. God and basically every soul I channel wants this for the living, so it is essential to understand, work through, and then make the best of what holds you back. I have an acquaintance named Bob who lost his wife to a stroke on a trip to the Bahamas. Ever since, taking any vacation, especially to a beach, is excruciating for him. He's a nervous wreck from the minute he books his flight, and this ruins his time away. So rather than simply travel less, Bob tries to work with his fear by going to a shore near his home—and when that fails, going camping with friends or for a hike instead. This way, he isn't far from support if he feels scared or uncomfortable. What matters to Spirit isn't whether Bob will ever enjoy the beach again, but that he knows he can't let life pass him by, because this will ultimately change him for the worse. To carry on, then, Bob's chosen to find ways to compensate for the effects of his trauma.

A therapist is more equipped to suggest ways to really deal with deep, fear-based grief responses than I am, but one thing I like to personally do when I feel a wave of grief coming on is to use it as a cue to stop, take a deep breath, and then tell a positive story about my loved one. So, for example, when I miss Gram, I find myself at an emotional crossroad. I can either feel anxious or afraid that nobody knows what to say or can relate to how I feel, or I can inject Gram's memory into a positive conversation. When a member of my crew was talking about his recent family vacation, I thought of how I used to camp with my grandparents, and a bunch of melancholy feelings about Gram bubbled up. So I shared how Gram would tuck me in at night in the top bunk of our camping trailer and how I loved waking up to the smell of her bacon, eggs, and French toast. I also told my crew how on our way to the campground, we'd use CB radios to communicate between my parents' and grandparents' cars. All of us kids had a handle, and mine was "Foxy Lady." Telling this story not only cracked us up but made me feel Gram's energy—and then, later that day, the wildest thing happened! I was killing time before a show, and I felt drawn to a candle I saw at a shop. I took a whiff and not only did the candle smell like gardenias—Gram's favorite flower—but the name of the fragrance was "Foxy Lady"! It was an insane validation that Gram wasn't just listening to my conversation, but appreciated how I chose to honor her in an uplifting way.

I'm sure you've caught on by now that Spirit likes to calm our sadness with a lighter perspective. After all, there are so many ways to look at a situation. To this end, Spirit says it's helpful to remember that waves don't just symbolize an emotional process that makes us feel unstable or caught unaware. There's a lot of beauty and purpose to waves too. They carry nutrients to marine animals along the shore, and move surfers and boats across the ocean. At the end of the day waves are part of the rhythm of life on this planet. They are part of God's design. And you know what? You are no different. You will encounter happiness, confusion, and loss many times. You too will rise and fall, rise and fall—just like the waves.

Healing Moments

Now that we all have water on our minds, I want you to create a positive message for your loved one, seal it in a bottle, and release it into a wavy ocean, sound, or sea. This can be anything from a love note or letter about your feelings to a small drawing, photograph, or some other cathartic form of expression that fits into the container. After you've let the bottle go, take in the moment with all your senses—smell the salty air, listen to the sound of the waves, and feel the sand between your toes. If you are not near a beach, you can instead bury the bottle in the ground and experience your surroundings using all your senses. In both cases, know that your loved one's soul is with you and has received your message loud and clear.

6

Faith and Prayer

My mama taught me to never talk about religion in public, but Spirit has no qualms about bringing it up on TV or in front of thousands of people at my live shows! That's because when you grieve, Spirit knows that having a faith and turning to practices like prayer and meditation can help you feel balanced, safe, and connected to a higher power. Since I'm Catholic, I call this energy God, but if that's too religious for you, God says you can simply call Him a higher power—whatever works. Personally, I don't care what you call God. Our source of creation is the same, no matter what the name. There is only One.

There's a lot to be said for believing there's a greater energy in charge of the world's rhymes and reasons, as unfair as they seem right now. The truth is, Spirit shows me that life is not arbitrary. Death, birth, sickness, and even a seemingly random traffic accident on the Long Island Expressway are part of a greater domino effect that occurs when your freewill choices combine with how the universe allows the day to go down. The reason Spirit encourages faith-based practices, prayer, and meditation, then, is because these tools help you connect with God and know that there is always purpose and hope.

You Gotta Have Faith

When I talk about having a faith, I never want people to think I'm out to convert anyone to mine, because I'm not. The only reason I like to publicly share my beliefs is to be open and honest—and demonstrate that I've learned how to marry my religious views with spiritual ones. Listen, I have Buddha statues all over my house, but I also have a Saint Theresa statue in my yard and rosary beads hanging from my bedroom mirror. I clearly believe there's no singular, "right" way to have a relationship with God.

Though God and religion are typically seen as being intertwined, they aren't the same thing. God is a positive, pure, and good entity, and religion is a set of beliefs and practices created to serve and worship God. You can use religion to follow God's ways, but He doesn't align Himself with one faith over another. I'm shown we are all connected to God, who is unconditional love, and it's that love which links us to our family and friends in the afterlife because we all come from His energy. God wants us to be part of a communal feeling of togetherness to help us feel less alone, particularly when we face loss.

Spirit encourages us to have a faith rooted in God because His teachings reinforce love and hope—and when we lose someone we care about, we lose our ability to see life through a positive lens. When a person dies, so many of our optimistic expectations get flushed down the toilet. A faith gives you something to hold on to and a reason to trust that things will turn around. It helps you feel encouraged that everything will be OK because the official creator of love and hope is rooting for you, especially when you're struggling. I'll never forget hearing a deacon say in his homily, "If you have even the slightest bit of faith, then you have hope, and if you have hope, you have love." Faith, hope, and love build on each other's momentum, and everything that's guided by these principles is stronger for it.

When Spirit tells me that a person who's grieving has lost all faith and doesn't know what to believe, I tell them it's OK—but if they can just believe that the souls of their loved ones are with them, that there's more to life than what's here in the physical world, and that the soul bond is never broken, these are stepping-stones to having faith. I think a lot of people who grieve turn from their faith because they feel God has let them down or taken a loved one from them. It's unfair and hard to accept that a loving, all-powerful figure would allow us to feel bad in any way. Listen, I get it. When I first realized I could talk to dead people, you better believe I got angry with God. I didn't ask for an ability that was demonized by my faith, and so I turned away from God for a long time because I didn't know what to believe. But I've learned how to incorporate faith in myself, faith in my religion, and faith in the unknown to make that work. I think it's the same thing with grief. You have to learn how that fits in with your faith in God. My situation didn't fit in with what I thought was true about God, and I had to reconcile that. You must do this for yourself too.

Spirit asks that we try to look at our grief with some perspective. I once read a fifteen-year-old girl who had lost her father and grand-father—she was so mad at God because she'd faced so much loss at a young age. Yet her grandfather stepped forward to acknowledge that while she's had many misfortunes, "you've also had many blessings. Even though you lost your father when you were very young, you had me." He went on to tell her that he knows her mom had just remarried, and she shouldn't feel guilty about calling him "Dad," because he was sent to play this role in her father's and grandfather's absence. He said that the next time she wonders why "God ruined her life," he wants her to consider how He's blessed it to compensate for the heartache she's felt. Spirit asked her to accept that the hardships we face in life have nothing to do with God's whim; they have to do with each soul's journey and its lifetime's purpose.

In addition to putting faith in God, you should also have faith in others and yourself. The best outcomes occur when you release your fears and doubts and move forward with faith. I realize that having faith isn't easy. It takes practice. You gain faith by using it and watching it work. So much of faith, then, is about trust. Trusting others and yourself. Trusting your journey, choices, and lessons. Believing there's a plan. Faith asks you to feel OK when you're falling apart. If you can just trust that you're being guided, that's faith. It isn't an empty-headed wish either—it comes with an instinctual sense that what you believe is true. That feeling comes from God, your angels and guides, and loved ones.

Dear God

Prayer is an act of communicating with God and Spirit, including souls of faith like saints or other deities, angels, guides, and your loved ones, and it can be a real boon as you grieve. Different faiths have different rituals for prayer, and God honors all of them if they're done with positive and pure intent. Just because I pray a Novena or the Rosary doesn't make me closer to God than you, and these prayers don't reach God any faster than yours. And while I also believe God is the greatest source of healing and providing, there are a lot of souls on the Other Side that work in conjunction with Him and can also "pick up the call"—though when you pray directly to God, I feel He's the only one who hears you. That being said, I don't think you need an official faith to pray. God honors your prayers if your intentions are pure.

Prayer is about asking God for what you desire and doing it with gratitude. Before I place a request, I thank God for the blessings in my life. I also don't use the words "I want" or "I need," though it's tempting! I ask God for His assistance or guidance with a situation and say "thank you" with the assumption that my requests are already on their way. Giving thanks before you receive a blessing implies that you have faith that the universe will deliver. I also like to be really specific, so I'm forced to nail down what it is that I need and Spirit can address it given the opportunities that are available in my life.

So let's say you crave support during grief, you might pray, "Dear God, thank you for all of my wonderful memories with Grandpa Frank who was such a huge part of my life, and for my family and friends who are doing their best to hold me up during this hard time. Thank you for also guiding me to a special friend who will know exactly what I'm going through so that we can help each other heal. . . ." Then you must keep an eye out for the answer to your prayer, which may not come in the package you expected. For example, the friend Spirit sends you might not share your faith or arrive on time for coffee dates. Stay open and say thank you, because there is likely a reason he or she was put in your path.

Spirit often says that although all our prayers are heard, they aren't always answered. This might feel like a kick in the gut, but the outcome of a situation may not be changeable or a frustration may be meant to teach a lesson to you or someone in your life. All you can do is have faith that your prayers will be addressed in a way that aligns with your lessons, growth, and God's intentions for your soul. Also keep in mind that because God gave you free will, you can't rely *only* on prayer without making an effort yourself! God's not your genie in a bottle, and prayer isn't Spirit's cue to give you what you want. I have a strong faith and know a lot about the Other Side, but Spirit doesn't run my life for me, and they won't run yours. They will intervene, assist, and guide you, but your life is what *you* make of it. Thanks to free will, your choices determine whether the majority of your time here is full of happiness or despair, confidence or fear, trust or doubt. This includes the decisions you make about how you grieve and heal.

Maybe right now, praying sounds too religious or you're not on speaking terms with God because you're upset that a loved one died; if so, a nice alternative to praying for what you desire is visualizing it. Visualizing your needs can also send a message to the Other Side about what you long for. All you have to do is close your eyes and imagine your heart's desire either playing out like a movie or even see it as a still image. The universe honors this because you're focusing on a want with a clear intention, similar to when you pray. To try visualization, sit quietly and surround yourself in white light and imagine anchoring yourself to the earth. Then paint a specific picture of what you'd like to transpire.

Finally, Spirit's told me that just thinking of loved ones and speaking to them is also a type of prayer because your positive and loving thoughts send them energy to help them on their journey on the Other Side. Be sure to thank them for their guidance and pray that their souls reach the highest attainable level of God's light and love. I like to think of it as giving back for all they do for us! I'll never forget hearing from a woman named Lois, who, at seventy-three years old, lost her seventeen-year-old grandson Jarred in a car accident. She and four family members came to my show in Fort Lauderdale, Florida. Lois said that when her grandson passed: "It was like nothing I have ever experienced. I couldn't function for at least six months. I would not see or talk to anyone, I stayed locked in my home. I screamed to the top of my lungs. I threw things. I ranted and raved like a lunatic. But at the same time, I knew he was safely with God." Lois was the last person to hug and kiss Jarred on her side of the family. "He didn't want to be hugged," she remembered, "but I said to him, 'Listen to me, I am your grandmother, and I may never live to see you ever again.' He hugged me so tight I thought I might bruise—I never thought he'd die first."

I didn't read Lois or her family, but after watching me channel others' loved ones, she said they felt peace that they'd not felt since her grandson's death, because they now knew that his soul was still with them—and ever since, Lois finds a lot of comfort in praying. "I do this everywhere," she said. "I just have normal conversations about how I miss him and always ask him to watch over his younger brother and dad. I laugh and remember things he did when he was younger. I cry and let him know that I'm sorry he won't know what it is to be a dad or in love. I talk to him in my thoughts and my heart but I know he hears me, and I believe I hear him." Last year on his eighteenth birthday, Lois's family had a private memorial service for Jarred. Lois had a hunch he'd want a birthday cake, so she bought him one and everyone sang happy birthday to his soul and blew out the candles. "That same day, I found a crystal angel earring that someone had lost," she marveled. "I really believe this was his way of thanking me."

Healing Moments

Before bed tonight, say a prayer to your loved one. This can be a faith-based prayer or more of a conversation about your day, how much you miss him, whatever you feel. Do this trusting that your loved one is safe and at peace with God and that Spirit hears every word and thought directed at them. If there is a prayer you really love that you want to remember and return to, write it in your journal or below.

7

Disbelief . . . or Spirit?

Even when a person has been ill, most of us have a knee-jerk reaction to the news that they've passed—we just can't fathom it. A lot like our body's startle or scratch reflexes, our heart seems to have an involuntary response to when death messes up our routine. Our minds can't catch up with reality, and so we default to a kind of comfortable fantasy. Grief counselors call this headspace "denial," which can be a confusing term. It's not that you don't *know* your loved one is dead. It's that you can't frigging believe it.

Spirit says that for most of us, disbelief is part reflex and part coping mechanism. You might involuntarily pick up the phone to tell your dad all about your day, forgetting he won't be there to answer, or expect your spouse to walk through the door at six p.m. like she used to, but then suddenly remember that's not happening. Or you might use disbelief as a survival skill. Rather than deal with a painful absence, it can be easier to imagine that your departed child is at school or your late brother is still at the hospital. You might even wake up every morning hoping and half believing that their death was a bad dream, even though you know this isn't really possible. No matter how your denial manifests, you will, in time, come to grips with the fact that the soul can only interact with you in spirit. Don't waste your time and energy denying this too. Embrace your new relationship for the amazing gift that it is.

Spirit says that what you think is denial may even be a soul connection. The reason you feel inclined to reach out to the departed might be because the soul is, in fact, near. You can't believe the person is gone because his soul didn't leave you. What you think is disbelief, then, isn't always generated in your mind; it may be an intuitive awareness. So when you feel inclined to call a friend who died or think you'll see your wife waiting for you in bed that night when you turn in, you may be sensing Spirit's presence. This isn't *always* the case, and I don't want you to live in a fantasy, but trust your gut when these moments occur. And rather than beat yourself up for feeling what you do, and assuming it means you're not healing, act on what you feel. Go on and talk to your loved one or even fluff up her pillow, but then move on to whatever you have to do next, just as you would if they were alive. Let the moment go.

Denial can have all three factors at play too. Nothing about grief is cookie-cutter or predictable! This was the case for a woman at a live show in Columbus, Ohio, named Hunter, who lost her fiancé, Blake, to pneumonia when he was just eighteen years old. Blake had an enlarged heart that was never diagnosed, but his asthma was, so when he began coughing like crazy, the couple thought it was the latter and didn't get him to the doctor until it was too late. What makes Blake's passing even harder is that Hunter was a certified medical assistant at the time, and she said she "hated herself" for not recognizing his symptoms earlier. Because she was angry at the situation and furious at herself, she also had very little patience for her two-year-old daughter Nathailee while she was grieving.

Though Hunter works hard to accept her partner's death, she still has moments of disbelief that Blake isn't with her. "He used to go out of town for work for days at a time, so it was normal for him to be gone," she said. "I feel like he's bound to come home soon, and I have to consciously remind myself that it's permanent." She's even left voice mails for him, forgetting he won't pick up. Her daughter Nathailee also knows that Blake's ashes hang around her mother's neck, yet she tends to yell his name as if he's just down the hall or around the corner. Hunter thinks this is mostly because Nathailee can't believe that he died, but she has seen her daughter speak to him as if he's in the same room, which also makes her think she sees his soul too. Blake hasn't left this little girl, and he remains close to the love of his life. As Blake's soul said, "Theresa, we were as thick as thieves. I'm not going anywhere."

Healing Moments

The next time you experience disbelief, call a friend or family member who's been there too. Sharing the moment can help you feel less bananas and alone. You don't have to make a big deal of it; just say, "I did the funniest thing today. It's been six years since Mom died, but I walked into the living room and felt like I was going to see her watching *Who Wants to Be a Millionaire?* Have you ever done something like that?" You'll talk about how the experiences made you feel, making it easier to move through them. You can always reach out to your loved one, as well. Close your eyes and visualize yourself, say, seeing Mom on the sofa and ask her who she thinks will win the final round of her show. This conversation may very well be her soul communicating with you from the Other Side; it may be just the salve you need.

8

Practice Calm to Carry On

"I don't know how to get through the day" is a concern I hear from a lot of my clients who are suffering. So much about grief involves listening and responding to your feelings, but it's important that you place equal emphasis on soothing yourself to calm some of that heartache too. This doesn't dishonor or disrespect your emotions or the person who passed but helps take some of the sting out of what you're going through, if just temporarily. And Spirit says you must give your mind, body, and soul occasional time-outs or they can't support you in the ways that you need. Without some breathing space from heavy, negative energy, for instance, your immune system takes a hit, your mind gets stuck in an anxious loop or clings to dark thoughts, and your soul begins to change in a critical way. The lower you feel and the longer you make this your emotional home base, the harder it is to lift yourself out of it. So please, don't misunderstand me—you are welcome to take the day off to feel lonely and upset, binge-watch *Grey's Anatomy*, and finish a sleeve of Chips Ahoy cookies (listen, there are worse ways to spend an afternoon!), but you must also build in time to comfort yourself in positive, healthy, and uplifting ways.

Soothing, of course, can mean different things to different people. Personally? I like to keep it simple. When you're grieving, everything already seems like too much work—from taking a shower to mailing a package—so inertia can set in and you can default to doing nothing at all. It seems so much easier to wait for a big project or opportunity to pull you out of your funk, though that day doesn't always come (and you might not even recognize it if it did). Better to devote what energy you have toward an activity that makes you feel a sigh of relief. This could be a diversion that feels like a treat of some kind, or if staying busy makes you feel good, accomplish a task that's easy but satisfying. Run a hot bath, water the plants, brush the dog, or make yourself blueberry pancakes for dinner. Right now, it feels like the world has turned upside down, so it's very important to be kind to yourself. This, at least, you can control.

Spirit adds that self-soothing is a nice way to both grieve and embrace life at the same time. This way, you don't deny how much you miss your loved one but you do admit how important it is to rejoin the living and take steps toward healing. Spirit is always with you as you do the things you love.

Spirit, Take Me Away . . .

Beyond the fact that it makes you feel good, what I love about self-soothing is that it teaches you to exercise choice over how you grieve, and in a gentle way that doesn't eat up too much of your time or energy. Choosing a simple, worthwhile task also reminds you that you are a person who can take initiative and deserves to feel complete. You don't have to stick to just one type of activity either; there are lots of options out there, and you should pick one based on what speaks to you when you crave it.

Because Spirit suggests that you grieve from the soul, most of your self-soothing activities can be chosen based on what you feel, when you feel it. Just because a cup of hot tea or a foot massage worked for you last week doesn't mean it will do the trick today. To respond to your soul's needs in the moment, it's as easy as asking yourself, *What can I do to feel good right now?* And then see how your gut responds. Its answer will come quickly and quietly, rising up from your most loving and truthful instincts. You can also schedule self-soothing activities according to the times of day that can be emotional sticking points for you. For example, if you tend to feel sad during dinner because you're not used to eating alone, maybe page through a book or watch a feel-good movie that'll raise your mood and energy level.

Remember, when you feel an instinctual nudge, this is often Spirit communicating with and through you. And as you heal, it is a soul's greatest hope that their messages will embolden you, especially when you're holding yourself back or getting in your own way. So if you think, *it's a pretty day to ride my bike into town . . .* that could be Spirit egging you on! Once I channeled a woman whose husband died two months prior; she was invited to a wedding but didn't feel like going. Then one day, she randomly thought, *I'm going to that wedding . . .* and when I channeled her husband's soul, he said it was his energy that told her to get out and enjoy herself. "If I were alive, we would go," he said. "It shouldn't matter that I'm no longer with you. Just because I died, you shouldn't stop living!"

Because Spirit wants the best for you, know that they won't encourage you to do things before your soul is ready. In fact, I find that instinctual prompts come in baby steps. So you might feel you could go to a party, but only for an hour. Or attend a wedding, but stay only for the service. And while you're there, check in with how you *feel*. If you're having fun, stay longer; if not, go home. Don't worry about looking pathetic or being rude to the host. How is leaving early in this case any less appropriate than if you didn't feel well from food poisoning? Do what you need to do, and don't worry about anyone else.

Go Easy on Yourself

Don't put a lot of pressure on the activities you choose. Especially when you aim to get things done, they do not need to have revolutionary, long-term effects or make sweeping changes in your home or community. Remember, the simple point of soothing pursuits is to make you *feel good*. That's it. Later, when your gusto returns, you can start a scholarship fund or nonprofit in a loved one's honor that changes the world. For now, it's enough to crawl into freshly washed sheets with a good podcast. If you're task-oriented, it might feel nice to accomplish a small duty like buying stamps or returning a friend's phone call. Maybe you can plant some tomatoes or sit on your favorite bench at the beach. So many of my clients think they have to landscape a whole garden or donate an expensive bench to honor loved ones and spend their time well. Who says? If an activity helps you feel even a slight release, it's done its job.

When you choose activities, go for healthy distractions and not ones that allow you to escape your feelings. There's a difference between seeing a movie that's engaging and getting lost in front of a dumb film you've seen a hundred times. Running away from your feelings takes you outside yourself and your soul; this leaves you further from knowing what you need in order to carry on. It is the opposite of healing.

I've seen a lot of my clients benefit from doing a relaxing activity that reminds them of a loved one or is something you did together. Organizing Grandma's old recipes because she loved hosting Sunday dinners or rereading emails from when you dated your late wife will bring on warm feelings—doing this under a cozy blanket or in front of a fire, even more so. A fan club member named Barbara who attended my live show in Utica, New York, lost her husband, Rick, of almost thirty-eight years to colon cancer. Barbara and her kids like to listen to the CDs that Rick used to play most often, including the Beatles, Katy Perry, and Aerosmith (I dig this guy's taste in music!). "The lyrics bring back the memories and moments we sang together," she told me. It also makes her feel good to kiss his picture every morning and night, and hug it when she sleeps. "Showing and giving love, hugs, and kisses were important to Rick. He was all about making everyone feel comforted, so I keep that up," she shared.

It's OK to Play

Self-soothing is all about you, and nobody else, so don't think about what others consider appropriate for someone in your state—believe it or not, this is a major consideration for my clients when deciding whether to infuse a little joy into their lives. Are you never supposed to feel a positive emotion again? Why are you letting others dictate when it's OK to cut yourself some slack? That's baloney. Your feelings are your business—done and done. I can't tell you the number of times Spirit tells clients to go to the movies or dance like crazy at a wedding, because these are things you loved doing prior to a loved one's death, and that shouldn't end. Spirit doesn't want you to stop being happy.

Oh, that reminds me of something else: No matter what your in-laws or that mouthy lady next door thinks, you aren't clinging to the past or disrespecting the dead by enjoying activities on your own that you once did with the deceased. In fact, your loved ones *want* you to soothe yourself with these memories because they lift your soul and the activities get you back out in the world again. I recently read a woman who lost her seventeen-year-old son in a car accident. She was still paralyzed with grief many years later, but her lingering sadness wasn't what her son's soul was worried about when I channeled him. In fact, he said, "It's OK that you still feel lost and numb, but I don't want you to stop yourself from doing things we loved to do because of what others will think." I don't mean to sound rude, but if I allowed what other people said about me to affect me—*she's a witch, she's a liar, who does she think she is with that big hair and those long nails*—I wouldn't be where I am today! Screw 'em.

Your loved ones aren't going to roll over in their graves if you put yourself before your grief for once; in fact, I wouldn't be surprised if they threw a little party in Heaven to celebrate! When I need to quiet my mind, I like to play loud music and zone out—whether it's Nora Jones or Nellie, it doesn't matter. And one time, I remember asking Spirit in this state, "When a person dies, you go to a funeral where you talk and tell stories that make you laugh or feel good. So why is it OK to express those happy feelings at a service but not at, say, a fortieth-birthday party a month later?" And you know what Spirit said? "No difference. Both are a gathering. Whether you're feeling content at a party or wake, it doesn't matter, because you're meant to celebrate life every day." There you have it. Straight from the horse's mouth.

Healing Moments

For one week, try to do a self-soothing activity every day or every other day, based on how you feel at the time or anticipate you'll feel during a consistently challenging part of the day. Again, these can be the tiniest of good-to-yourself efforts, like eating a banana with almond butter to boost your energy, buying yourself a bright pink dahlia to put on your nightstand, taking a barefoot walk in the grass. After each, write in your journal about how the activity made you feel. Consider reusing the ones that made you feel good in the future, and scrap the ones that left you indifferent or empty. You'll learn a lot about what you need, and what it takes to feel satisfied in your new normal, by being mindful during this process.

9

There's No Place Like Om

I know that not everyone is into prayer or faith-based practices, so I want to talk for a minute about meditation as another way to help you process grief, find some peace, and connect with your loved ones' souls. You can also meditate in addition to praying; it doesn't have to be an either/or scenario. Meditation is soothing and peaceful, and when your heart is in turmoil, it's a real gift to yourself to take a moment to breathe. I find that meditation drains away all negativity so I can feel what's in my soul. I hope the same for you, and that this quiet time will reveal what you further need to heal your pain.

Your Time, Your Way

To meditate, you'll want to find a quiet space where you can be alone and clear your mind—in your yard, at a pretty scenic overlook, in the sauna at the gym . . . wherever you feel safe and serene. I like to meditate in my bedroom once a day, and I usually light a candle to mark the beginning of the practice. You can create whatever rituals you'd like—putting a favorite blanket over your shoulders or wearing a piece of your loved one's jewelry—that will help to free you from anxiety and connect with Heavenly thoughts. You could even arrange a few stones in front of you that have uplifting sayings about healing printed on them, or light an aromatherapy candle whose essential oils are known to support the grieving process. Sandalwood, cinnamon bark, frankincense, myrrh, grapefruit, chamomile, rose, and lavender are just a few fragrances with soothing and healing properties for those who are moving through loss.

Before you meditate, you must first protect and ground yourself in God's white light. This keeps away any negative energy or souls while you're in this state. To do this, some clients like to picture themselves in an egg-shaped or circular bubble; I like to visualize my body outlined in white light. I also visualize all gray negativity leaving my physical, emotional, and spiritual body and being replaced with pure, white light. I then ground myself to the earth by imagining two cords from the bottoms of my feet, and one from my tailbone, shooting into the earth and locking them in like the roots of a tree.

During your actual meditation, choose an objective that speaks to what you're feeling in that moment. You can sit quietly with your eyes shut to help clear your head if you're on overdrive, focus on your breath with a hand on your heart if you want to show yourself compassion, or ask your loved one's soul a question and sense a response if you need guidance. You can also focus on a positive word or phrase ("I will make choices that help heal my soul") or on what your body is doing (breathing, hearing, feeling, smelling . . .) as you concentrate on the present moment. If you sense that you have a lot of pent-up feelings to release, you can also just sit quietly and allow them to flow out of you—pain, anger, love, fear, sadness, whatever you're bottling up inside. Do not consciously try to think about your sad experience to cause a reaction, but let your emotions drive the meditation, allow them to reach their peak on their own, and feel them fade away. Meditation can cause an energetic release, so if you feel a good cry coming on, don't hold back. If you'd like a little more structure or variety to your meditations, you can find great self-guided meditations online or on iTunes that specifically focus on grief and healing.

For me, meditation is a nice way to be quiet and focused enough to hush my mind while hearing what Spirit has to say. You can be quiet and focused while praying too, but prayer is *talking* to God, whereas meditation lets you *listen* to God and other Heavenly souls, including your loved ones. It gives you access to the universe and connects you with Spirit by linking your soul to those on the Other Side. And while you don't have to be a medium to experience soul communication, you aren't guaranteed to see a full-blown apparition of Uncle Pete during your meditative moment either. What is the best way to feel tranquil and fulfilled both during and after meditation? Set your expectations aside and simply receive.

Healing Moments

When I miss my loved ones, I like to do a calming beach meditation. Why don't you give it a try? It doesn't matter if you don't consider yourself a visual person; listen, when I close my eyes, I only see dark. So to begin, shut your peepers and picture yourself surrounded by white light and then ground yourself to the earth like I talked about. Visualize yourself sitting on a beach—you can be in a chair or on the sand . . . it doesn't matter. Now look out across the water. Hey, it's a boat! Notice that the boat is approaching you and, as it comes closer, there are people on it. Who do you see? Nine times out of ten, it's your loved ones and/or your angels and guides. If for some reason your boat is empty, don't sweat it. Take a deep breath, ask your loved ones to jump on board next time, and try again tomorrow.

When I do this exercise, for some reason I see a pirate ship. And as it draws closer to shore, I can see my departed grandparents and uncle waving at me. They always look healthy and happy, and I wave back like my hand's going to fall off. Sometimes I let the ship come up to the beach and I meet them for a hug. It's the best feeling in the world, because I know that I'm not making it up. Spirit loves this meditation as a way to connect with loved ones in Heaven, and says that what you envision is real.

Draw or write about what *you* see below.

10

Let's Talk Destiny

"When it's your time, it's your time" may sound like a cliché, but it is actually a spiritual truth. Spirit insists that our destinies are set. Our souls have a determined period of time on earth to live, learn, and love—and then a window of time, not an exact date, during which it will bid *arrivederci*. Is that window a few weeks, months, or years? I have no clue. What I do know is the time frame might've been determined by your soul before you were born or chosen according to lessons your soul or those around you need to learn. And while your brain has no idea when you'll depart, your soul always does and carries this information with it. The soul also lets your body and life choices dictate how you pass, maybe to stress the point that up until the end, our lives on this plane are defined by our free will. In the meantime, God wants you to live each day to the fullest, never afraid or held back by what's to come.

Timing Is Everything

Spirit really drives home the concept of destiny when the person I'm reading feels a death could have been prevented—if the doctor had caught the tumor sooner, if the person had stayed home from work, if you'd been driving the car that night, and so on. But there are a few categories of "how I died" scenarios that illustrate the destiny point best and that Spirit says is clear proof that we aren't in control of our end.

For one, "near miss" anecdotes do a good job reinforcing that you have a predetermined time on earth, because they demonstrate that threatening incidents outside your destiny window don't cause death; they just become part of your story that hopefully serves to help, teach, or encourage others in some way. It's like the story I read about a student named Victoria McGrath who became famous for surviving the Boston Marathon bombing when her leg was ripped apart by shrapnel just five feet from the finish line. Victoria became a public face of hope and survival, thanks to an iconic photo of her being carried to safety by medics who saved her legs. "I don't know why I was so lucky in this case," she even told the *Today* show. Cut to three years later, when Victoria died as the passenger in a car crash in Dubai. Her friend, the driver, was zooming along in a yellow Ferrari and smashed into a lamppost, tearing the car in half. If you can believe it, he actually posted a picture on Facebook with his new sports car shortly before the fatal accident with the caption "Picked up the Ferrari. Don't worry, I won't speed ;)." Spirit showed me that it wasn't Victoria's time to pass when she used her free will to run a marathon and was hurt in the bombing, but once she hit her destiny window, her free-will choice to ride in that car defined the very tragic means by which she died.

Unforeseen or freak accidents also point to destiny windows, especially when they occur in situations that a person has already faced without consequence. I once channeled the souls of three men who died while sailing on a lake. Their boat's anchor rope became tangled, which caused the vessel to flip over when a wave struck. It toppled all three men, who drowned. Two bodies were found days later, and one was still missing when I read the family. Yet when I channeled these happy-go-lucky souls, they insisted they'd done this a million times and wouldn't have gone out if they'd thought it was dangerous. They were confident and, even up to the end, having a good time trying to tackle their boating challenge!

Our souls can also make death-related arrangements either before they come to earth or at various points during the lives of those involved. This last one always amazes me because it implies that your soul can somehow act and communicate independent of your body and brain while you're still alive! I've seen this happen when, say, a husband's soul opts out early in its destiny window because the man's death was taking too hard a toll on his caretaker, and I've also been told about how souls determine who will carry the greatest burden connected to a departure, if multiple people are involved. This last one happens a lot with children's deaths, actually. I remember a few times that a child died in the hands of someone other than the person I was reading—like with an ex, at a daycare, or with in-laws—because everyone's souls in the scenario agreed to ease the burden for the person who'd feel it the most.

Don't get me wrong: Knowing you have a set destiny doesn't give you permission to live recklessly or ignore your health, happiness, and well-being! If you do, you'll only live out the rest of your years feeling like crap or with the ramifications of your behavior. But believing in a destiny should convince you there's never anything you can do to prevent a departure. If your loved one didn't die that day in a plane crash because he'd taken a train, it still doesn't mean he would have lived to be a hundred years old. He may have just passed from a sudden heart attack a few months later.

When Choices Come with Burdens

It can be hard to wrap your head around the fact that we don't cause our ultimate death, but we do make choices and decisions that determine how we die. And if it is hurtful to others in some way, Spirit will usually apologize during a reading for how they passed. But Spirit taking accountability is not Spirit saying that had they made different choices, they would have lived past that point. In the end, there is no "good" way to die, short of helping others or after having a homemade lasagna. What we really want is that our loved ones made no choices at all, so death would never occur, which of course is not possible.

When poor choices cause a death, those left behind usually struggle, so Spirit tries to help them heal by explaining that destiny trumps everything. During a live show in Newark, I read a mom whose son, as the driver, survived a car accident though his two friends, as passengers, died. When I channeled the souls, I said to the son, "They do not blame you in any way for what happened. They said, 'We all made choices that day. And we did crazier things on other days and nothing happened.' " They didn't want the friend who lived to have survivor's guilt, because "it wasn't your time to leave." The young man's soul was meant, instead, to learn from the situation—perhaps self-love or gratitude for his life.

It may be hard to believe, but Spirit's also revealed that the destiny window applies to tragic suicides. Some mediums insist self-inflicted deaths are an exception to the rule—that if you choose to end your life, you're using free will to cut your journey short. I used to assume this too, but my guides have now confirmed otherwise. Lately I've paid closer attention to this point and seen for myself that they're right—only a few suicides happen before a destiny, but most occur within a block of destined time. So it's only when a person's free-will choice occurs in its destiny window that the attempt "sticks," for lack of a better term. For instance, I once channeled the soul of a man who jumped out a window but lived fifteen more years in a wheelchair, only to pass from a health issue. I also think of a woman who tried six different ways to exit this earth, but it wasn't until her seventh attempt that she died. Another heartbreaking example is that of a son whose mother happened to walk in when he was about to cut his wrists—

therefore saving him from this terrible scenario—yet a few years later, he died from an accidental drug interaction with Benadryl. There's the other side of the coin too, where I channeled a young man who hung himself, but said it *wasn't* intentional. I remember saying to his soul, "How do you want me to tell your mother and sister that you did not die on purpose, but you put a rope around your neck and passed?" He explained that he was fighting with his girlfriend and told her that if she didn't come to the house to talk, he'd commit suicide. So he staged a hanging as a threat, but after waiting for an hour or so, the woman never showed. As the young man went to step off the chair, he slipped and got caught in the noose. Though the autopsy results confirmed that the position of the rope proved it wasn't an intentional suicide, my guides said it was the boy's time to pass. So regardless of what one's free-will choices are that bring about a departure, you don't depart unless your soul has fulfilled its journey.

Healing Moments

Neither you nor your loved one's soul can do anything to change destinies that are predetermined before we come to this plane. So what *can* you do something about? Set a timer for eleven minutes—this is a very spiritual number related to angelic guidance and protection—and think about what you need from your life that you can control. Maybe you want to wake up without anxiety, find the patience to raise your kids while also mourning, or let go of the fear that your loved one isn't with God. Spend eleven positive minutes visualizing what this desire would look and feel like, and when the timer goes off, say, "I give this hope to God. Please show me opportunities that will help make it happen." And then take them!

11

The Soul Lives On

My clients are always concerned that their loved ones just go away forever when their lives end. They worry about whether that person will be remembered by others, and in what way. They wonder what their role is in keeping their loved one's memory alive, and how the soul might be interacting with them each day. They become overly concerned that they're not doing enough to honor them, or that they're doing too much. It's a crazy-making mind game, and I want to help put it to bed.

As you know, a loved one's soul will always be in your life in spirit form. The question, then, isn't *if* your loved one will be remembered—trust me, they'll send you so many signs that you couldn't forget them if you tried!—but what part you'll play in the soul's existence as it moves ahead on its journey. Over the years, Spirit has talked about three main ways that souls keep on participating in your life. Are there more than three? Oh, I'm sure there are! Spirit's abilities are limitless and go way beyond what they have time to tell me during a reading. The following are those that will help you heal the most.

#1 Spirit Makes Itself Part of Your Life

OK, the first and most common way souls live on is by experiencing earth again with us. Spirit loves to show me two ways that they do this. So let's say you decide to go to the park for the afternoon. First, your loved one can participate *alongside you* in soul form, which we've already discussed a bit. So while you sit on a bench at the park, their soul might come along but play on the swings and slides; or if you decide to fly a kite at the park, they might sit under a tree to watch you embrace the day. Second, souls have the amazing ability to experience events *through you*. They don't jump into our bodies to feel what we do—no weird, horror-flick shenanigans here. But to use the park example, they can watch an event play out like a movie, and then through your eyes experience what you're seeing, feeling, thinking, and more. Either way, if you invite a soul to join you on an outing, it definitely will. Spirit always says this is one of their favorite things to do with us, since they never stopped enjoying time with you.

One of my favorite stories about how loved ones' souls hang out with us is one I heard from my client Marisa. The night before she was to give a talk at a computer conference, she had a dream about her father, who'd died two years earlier. In the dream, Dad was smiling and drinking a cup of coffee while wearing a Hawaiian shirt in the middle of what felt like a paradise. He looked happy and healthy, surrounded by apple trees, a peach tree, and lush plants. When Marisa woke up, the dream made her so happy that she decided to "use" her warm memory from the night before at her speaking engagement. During her talk, Marisa imagined that her dad was in the audience and that she was talking only to him. This eased her mind, and she did a great job. Afterward, Marisa bought herself a coffee in the lobby and couldn't believe it when the barista was the spitting image of her dad—similar fashion sense, same glasses, recognizable demeanor, and both spoke Spanish! With tears in her eyes, Marisa asked the man for a cappuccino with skim milk. "Fat free?" he asked. "Go through life with whole milk!" This freaked Marisa out, since these words were exactly what her father used to say when she'd ask him to buy skim milk for her coffee! The encounter felt so familiar and real that Marisa began to cry. "*Fine*," the man said. "I will get you skim milk." These too are the words and tone her dad used when he'd give in to her request!

Little did this guy know that Marisa's tears were a mix of sadness and joy, because she sensed that having the dream about her father, feeling him in the audience, and ordering a coffee from his practical twin were signs that his energy was with her all day. When Marisa told me this remarkable story, I immediately knew she'd made him very proud, and that her father sent her the barista as a validation that he lived her speech through her eyes and, in that way, was indeed at the conference with her.

#2 Souls Reincarnate in Others

The second way a soul can live on is to reincarnate in your lifetime. This doesn't happen a lot, so when it does, it's really special. Once in a blue moon, the entire soul can come back in another body (this mostly happens with miscarriages, infants, and young kids) or, more commonly, a part of the soul can become part of another person in the form of, say, a physical trait or familiar mannerism. I'll never forget when I first read my client Summer, who tragically lost her daughter shortly after she was born. Summer's water broke after forty happy, easy weeks of pregnancy, and labor was straightforward and normal until it was time to push. Suddenly, her daughter Season's heart stopped beating for unknown reasons. Season was immediately given oxygen and CPR, but it took at least twenty minutes to bring about a faint heartbeat. The family was then rushed to Seattle Children's Hospital, where the best doctors did everything they could to save Season. She received daily blood and plasma transfusions and medications to help her blood pressure stabilize, and was fully intubated. Her family watched her numbers rise and fall, obsessing over every bit of news. Her first MRI came back perfect and showed no brain damage, and the family held out hope that her organs, including her kidneys, which were filling with fluid, would start to work again. The edema, or massive fluid retention, however, forced Season to be put on life support. From there, every day was a strenuous battle for that baby to stay alive. When her second MRI showed extensive brain bleeds, followed by an equally bad CT of her bowels, Season's body decided it was done after fighting for thirty-three days. Her extended family gathered around Season and held her as they said their good-byes.

During Summer's reading, Season's beautiful soul explained that most of her mother's healing would occur when an aspect of her soul became part of a little sister. Summer gave birth to Gem almost exactly a year after Season. Summer calls Gem a "rainbow baby," a term given to an infant who arrives after the loss of a beloved child and brings so much light after darkness. In fact, when I channeled Season, she said to her mom, "When you look at [Gem's] eyes, you'll see the life in *my* eyes." Sure enough, Summer says that when she looks in Gem's magical dark eyes, she does in fact see her daughter Season shining through. I don't think it's any coincidence that one's eyes are also the window to the soul.

#3 Their Soul Is Now Part of You

Spirit says your loved one's energy can live on through *you*—your personality, behavior, and a readiness to help others in a way that you know would make your loved one proud or reminds you of something they'd do. Spirit often says, "My handprint will always be on your heart," or "You carry me in your heart every day"—and this is more than a feel-good epithet. I'm shown that loved ones leave an actual part of their souls in this world with you—an energetic imprint, or handprint, that lives inside you (in your heart or soul). This could be a feeling, memories, or even specific behaviors. When you share good times with another living being (including animals) or act or speak in a way that another person has taught you, a part of that person's energy literally becomes part of yours. A simple example is how you might hum while chopping vegetables like your late sister always did, or use a phrase that you picked up as a child and think, *That's so Mom of me.* The memories you carry are also energetic, so when you share "Remember when?" stories about your loved one, know that you are experiencing their energy too.

As you carry a soul's imprint with you, be sure you're honoring your loved one in a positive way because this also leaves a mark on our world. Help their best legacy to go on. One of the more moving things I've heard Spirit say is, "I don't want how I died to define the person I was in the physical world." Your loved ones don't want you to focus on how they passed but celebrate the best version of their lives. Keep these words in mind when you worry about how others look back on your loved ones too: *Will my sister's friends treasure that she was a good mom and volunteered at the hospital . . . or just that she died from pancreatic cancer? Will my son's classmates remember that he was a baseball star and great big brother . . . or will they focus on the overdose that ended his life?* Don't think twice about what goes on in other people's heads, but always reinforce all the good your loved ones have done in the world.

You need to know too that God and your loved ones are exceptionally moved when a soul has become such a big part of you that you're moved to help others in their name. This is like how Summer, who lost her baby in the earlier story, found that the trauma of living in the hospital for some time, and losing her child, made her family want to help others in their shoes. When they were at the hospital, they often felt the need to be near but also to take a breath of fresh air during procedures for which they couldn't be present. So Summer launched Season of Miracles Foundation, which is currently designing a healing sanctuary at Seattle Children's Hospital for families to wish, pray, heal, or even grieve. The sanctuary will have a water fountain, colorful artwork, gazebo for privacy, reflexology path, and other healing features. Frankly, I can't wait to visit it myself! "We did this out of love for our daughter," Summer said. "We heal by telling Season's story in a way that helps others and doesn't allow her to be forgotten."

Healing Moments

Make time for an activity that your loved one's soul couldn't resist! During your outing, imagine that your loved one's soul is either with you or experiencing this through your eyes. Don't make their presence an obsessive focus, but gently keep it in the back of your mind. When you get home, take out your journal and either write about how the day made you feel or draw a picture of what transpired and include your loved one's soul in it. (Stick figures are great. You think I can sketch like Picasso?) If you released a balloon in Pop's honor, for example, would he be standing next to you, floating above you, or holding on to the string as it sails away? Know that if you felt Spirit's presence at any point, it was real.

12

What's Heaven Like?

Even if you aren't sure that you believe in an afterlife, you probably wonder about Heaven once in a while—OK, maybe *a lot*. Does it exist, and are your loved ones there? What does it look like? What do souls do all day? Do they ride on unicorns, float around like Casper, or walk on those streets of gold we hear so much about? I've been asked all these questions and more by clients, and you're not crazy for thinking about this topic either! Listen, if someone you cared about took a trip or moved to another country, you'd naturally wonder where they were, what they were doing, and how they felt. So of course you can't stop thinking about your loved one's new home—they're in another *realm,* for Pete's sake.

Spirit encourages us to believe in an afterlife, because trusting there's a Heaven implies knowing there's a higher power and a place for your loved one's soul. Spirit often says, "Tell my mom/sister/dad/ friend there is a God" or "I'm with God now," because at the heart of all skepticism about the Other Side is the concern that our souls just float around some unfamiliar place when we die, by themselves, if they go anywhere at all. It's about a fear that there is no God and that all the details of our lives are arbitrary and meaningless. Bringing up Heaven, then, is your loved one's way of telling you where they are, who they're with, and preparing you for what's to come. It reinforces that someday you'll be together again, and in the meantime, that life on earth is purposeful and was created by God.

A Heavenly View

I believe that Heaven is very close to our realm, but not everyone can see it. When I'm shown a glimpse of the Other Side, I feel as if it's right here with me—not above us in the sky or way beyond the stars. God's energy is among us too. To me, Heaven is almost like a sheet of tissue paper that's placed over our physical world. There are also additional dimensions that go deep, not up, like in movies where they open a door and there's another world on the opposite side, except there's no doorway to step through. When souls are about to cross over, they can see that our worlds kind of coexist and are not afraid. It's a temporary separation for us, but not so much for them because they get to experience our plane when they want.

To understand how I interpret Heaven as it's shown to me, it helps to understand the extent of what I usually channel. I'm empathic, which means I mostly feel Spirit and its surroundings and then use my other senses to fill in the blanks. I receive impressions, similar to a quick thought that flashes in my mind, along with any other quali- ties—smells, sounds, emotions, physical feelings—that are related to them. I rarely see things in a visual way, with the exception of shadows and silhouettes that fade in and out. So when Spirit refers to Heaven, they only show me glimpses that fit this framework and the soul I'm channeling. I might sense a child playing on swings and feel the wind in her hair or feel I'm in a loving space surrounded by laughter but visually see nothing at all. I think I'm only shown certain aspects of the Other Side because I'm not meant to know everything yet, and I'm good with that. I don't push Spirit on this topic. My job is to share my experiences and help those who grieve. That's my purpose, and I stick to it.

So when I channel loved ones, I don't climb a set of cloudlike stairs toward a bright light or see angels floating around playing harps! Spirit actually brings me to a calm waiting area where all the souls go in order to communicate with me—a kind of gathering place. Here, it feels very peaceful and reminds me of the final scene in *Ghost* when the character Sam finally crosses over and the background becomes white; all you can see are the faint silhouettes of different souls lined up behind him. I've come to think of this space as a part of Heaven, the way a nice foyer is a room in a much bigger home.

During meditation, Spirit has also brought me to a few scenic spots on the Other Side, but I'm not sure where they are relative to the rest of Heaven. I've visited a bright and airy environment near a babbling brook and crystal-clear waterfall, since water is thought to help you connect with Spirit. H_2O is a very powerful, intuitive element, and I don't think it's a coincidence that up to sixty percent of the human adult body is water. I do a lot of hovering in these celestial locations too. I gently float above the rocks near a stream and over fields and playgrounds. I'm never strutting around on a solid surface, but coasting a few inches above it. Maybe that's why shoe shopping feels like such a treat in this world!

I've also come to suspect that while Heaven feels the same for everyone—an overwhelming sense of the deepest, purest love—it looks different to each soul and is very personal. I think the Heaven you see and experience is partly based on what's familiar to you, maybe from your faith or upbringing, or is comforting to think about. It's these thoughts that influence your surroundings. So if you're Catholic, you may see streets of gold and pearly gates, or if you've read a lot of new age books, maybe light beings in white robes milling around a Grecian building. Hey, if it were up to me, Heaven would look like my bedroom! When I recently spruced it up, I did this with the hope that it would look like "a little piece of Heaven." So we installed a white shag carpet, white curtains, white comforter, white dresser and side tables, and used swirly white wallpaper on my ceiling. I also have a chair that's as blue as the sky, and the interior of my walk-in closet is gold! I could stay in my new bedroom all day. It feels so cozy and safe.

And while God and I probably have different tastes when it comes to decorating, I do have it on good authority that Heaven's atmosphere makes every soul feel secure and at ease. My friend Regina, whose son Brian died in a drowning accident and was the first child I ever channeled, gets regular visits from Brian's soul, so I asked Regina if Brian ever had anything to say about Heaven. What's crazy is that the day before I reached out about this, a friend of Brian's godmother coincidentally saw another medium, and Brian came through like gangbusters with a special message about the afterlife! In fact, Regina told me, "Brian's already shown me Heaven in my dreams, and he's made sure I know he's happy and at peace. I believe he knew *you* wanted to hear about Heaven and couldn't wait to help! He timed it just right, to make the book more interesting." In fact, Brian was pumping his fist—which he used to do when he felt really joyful— and throwing his shoes in the air and smiling, which is how he'd settle in after a long day. Brian said, "Everything is OK in Heaven! It feels very open and light here." By pumping his fist and tossing his shoes, Brian was adding that he's happy and at home.

When Regina heard about Brian's message, she felt her son's presence (Regina is very intuitive). He had his arms around her back, and she could feel Brian gently patting it, just like he would when he was alive. Through dreams, Regina's been shown that her son's Heaven is colorful and vibrant. "Brian loves nature and animals," she said. "His favorite place is under a flowering tree, on a hill overlooking fields of wild flowers, lakes, and waterfalls. All of our pets that have passed away are with him." She also knows Brian is with his father, Bill, who died about twelve years later; this brings her tremendous comfort.

Keeping Busy

In Heaven, souls spend time doing what they loved on this plane—cooking, dancing, playing tennis—but they also do meaningful work to help humans, grow their own souls, and learn lessons. This doesn't always come up in readings, so I want to share a few jobs with you because I think they're pretty neat.

One of the most important jobs on the Other Side is that of a "greeter." When you cross you're met by a loved one, but you might also meet a greeter soul who died in a similar way. Their job, then, is to let the new soul know they're not alone in how they passed; it reassures them that everything will be OK as they transition to Heaven. Children often greet other kids who die young, for instance, especially if they loved or worked with kids in this world. This is like a client who'd given birth to a stillborn and then went on to have eight (eight!) miscarriages. Spirit told me that her first child greeted all of its siblings and unrelated stillborns too. Don't worry, the story has a happy ending—she went on to have healthy twins! I also remember reading a woman whose sister was murdered, and her soul became a greeter of others who passed in a similar way. I've channeled greeters of those who share an interest, as well, like a young boy who was a camp counselor on earth and loved coaching sports like baseball. His job was to greet kids in Heaven and teach them to play all kinds of sports on the Other Side for fun!

Another fascinating job is that of a teacher. Because your soul is always striving to reach higher levels of learning, much of a soul's time is spent choosing and preparing for the lessons it will learn in its next life. To this end, I remember reading a woman whose departed daughter was a teacher on the Other Side; her "lesson plans" involved prepping souls on how they'd mature their spirits before incarnating.

In Good Company

As I've mentioned, your loved ones are not alone on the Other Side. They're with the souls of those who died before them, plus angels and spirit guides from their many lifetimes. If the soul had a strong faith in the physical world, Spirit might also show me they're with a faith-based deity that either they, or you, value like saints, the Blessed Mother, Buddha, whoever. This further supports my belief that Heaven is at least partly related to what brings you or a soul peace. For instance, I could read two different people who believe in Jesus and see two different versions of him. So if one person grew up Catholic and surrounded by little religious statues in their house, I might see a figurine of the Infant of Prague—a sixteenth-century Roman Catholic interpretation of Jesus. But if another client were raised in a different Christian faith, Jesus's soul would likely appear as a more mainstream depiction—say, an adult man with long, dark hair and a beard. What matters is that you trust that the deity, in this case Jesus, is with your loved one.

Spirit's Got the Look

Spirit can take on different appearances because in Heaven we don't need bodies; we exist as souls made of a brilliant white light. Like the Jesus example, however, your loved ones' souls show themselves to me with distinguishing characteristics that will resonate with you—maybe dressed like they appear in a photograph you like or as a younger version of themselves during a time when they were happy. This makes me think of a man named Ken who, with his wife, Molly, won a VIP trip to attend my live show in Macon, Georgia, and have dinner with me and the crew. Afterward, we spent some one-on-one time together, which is when Ken blew my mind with a story about how a family member's soul showed up at his deceased mother's funeral, dressed to impress in a way that reflected a cherished family photo.

So when Ken's mom passed away, he wrote a letter to her soul that he read at her service. Just before he began, he asked everyone there to hold up silk bluebonnets that had been distributed in her honor. From his vantage point at the podium, it was such a pretty site that Ken set his camera on the stand to take a photo at the widest view he could achieve. When Ken got home later, he downloaded the picture to his computer and noticed two crazy things about it. First, there was an incredible silhouette of what appears to be a brightly lit angel with a blue aura in the back of the church. But even more insane was the figure of a woman in a white-collared dress and red hair, leaning against a wall of windows off to the side. In real life, it would be impossible for a human being to stand in this location because the church's pews backed up to the wall with no room for anyone to stand up! And by the way, neither the angel nor the woman appeared in a video recorded at the same time. They only appear in Ken's fascinating photo.

Though Ken and his wife, Molly, didn't know who the woman in the picture was at the time, Molly figured it out when she later stopped by her deceased mother-in-law's house. There, she noticed a picture on the wall from 1909 with a woman who looked just like the one in the back of the church! It turned out to be Ken's grandmother when she was fourteen years old. A few months after, Ken ran across his grandmother's obituary and read that his mom *and* grandmother were buried on the same day in March, thirteen years apart! I believe Grandma was at her daughter's funeral, appearing in a recognizable way.

Finally, it's important to know that since a soul is made entirely
of light, all pain, disability, and illness are left with the physical body
when the soul leaves it. Spirit loves to demonstrate this during readings! The once immobile jump up and down. Those with no teeth
flash their now-gorgeous smiles. All souls channel with personality
and laughter, because it's the best medicine for your soul and if they
were in a bad place, they wouldn't be able to make jokes! They also
make me feel like the second the soul pulls out of the body, they
experience a much-needed release—almost like air coming out of a
balloon. Suddenly, Spirit says they feel "light and free." One of the
more gruesome stories I've ever channeled demonstrates how ravaged
a body can be, yet when the soul crosses over, it still exists in a healthy
and happy form on the Other Side. At a live show, I read a woman
whose sister was murdered by a family friend who tried to take advan-
tage of her, and when she fought back, he hurt her, left her for dead,
and then moved her body to a deserted area. The soul actually made
me feel a blow to the head, and *my* body being moved and scraped
against the concrete. I felt flesh wounds, marks around my neck,
scratches, and like my skin had been torn off by wild animals. I could
even feel my body decomposing. Listen, this was not a pretty reading,
and the family had felt tortured by the details of this departure since
the police found the woman's body. But that's why the soul needed
me to update them! The woman's magnificent, light, and happy soul
floated forward to insist that she did not suffer—it left the physical
body the minute she was knocked out—and that she's healthy, whole,
and worry-free in Heaven. It took *a lot* of energy for her to communicate these details, which tells me her soul is also very strong.

Healing Moments

Relaxed and with your eyes closed, I'd like you to envision your loved ones in Heaven. What does it look like there? What are they doing? Who are they with? Whether the images come to you in a flash and then disappear, or linger in your mind's eye, Spirit says they are purposeful and a very real glimpse of the Other Side. Be aware too of any feelings or sensations that you experience—a light and airy feeling, overwhelming calm, chills, maybe even a sense that your loved one is sitting beside you. Trust your intuition that these are messages from your loved one's soul and a peek into where they now call home.

13

Read the Signs

I absolutely love talking about signs and symbols, because they pack such a fascinating one-two punch. First of all, it's amazing to consider that a loved one's energy can send you signs at all, and then to think they're actually communicating through these means? *Kapow!* Mind. Blown. I always say, if anything goes on around you that seems odd, weird, different, or like a coincidence—and these things also make you think of a loved one or remind you of that person—please embrace it as a sign that the soul is with you at that exact moment. What's even cooler is that the more you acknowledge signs and use them to help you heal, the more signs Spirit will send you, because you'll know how these souls operate *and* you'll have also signaled to Spirit that you're all ears! As I've said before, you share a bond with your loved ones that can never be broken, and they're just as interested in reaching out to you as you are to them.

Show and Tell

Spirit sends signs for all kinds of reasons. Mostly, your loved ones do this to comfort, reassure, and guide you. They want you to know they're with you, while at the same time experiencing a joyful existence that coexists with our plane. Spirit also hopes signs will reinforce your belief in an afterlife, which is where its soul now exists. It's easy to fear what you can't anticipate, so by interacting with you through signs, Spirit is showing you there's nothing to dread about their death or yours. In fact, this is their way of demonstrating that someday you'll interact with the living the same way they do with you! Finally, if you're worried that a soul is upset about being dead or didn't make it to Heaven because of, say, how the person died, Spirit uses signs to tell you they're safe and at peace. Before I honed my abilities, I thought souls must feel lost and tortured without their loved ones and have this pained need to communicate like in the movie *Ghost*. Remember how Sam's soul was constantly yelling at his wife, *I'm right here! Why don't you see me?* But that's not the reality. Spirit says that from the moment the soul leaves the physical body, it feels tons of love and safety, and knows it will interact with you again, just in a different way.

To receive signs, you don't have to do anything other than become aware of them. Spirit already sends you signs all day long, but if you're grieving too hard or are distracted by other negative stressors, you may not notice. At a live show in Newark, New Jersey, I channeled a husband who died by accidentally mixing his meds, and his soul put me in a hallway with three bedrooms and a bathroom. He then showed me that he actually passed through this area as a shadow, and that his friend saw it while his wife didn't. The problem is, when she heard the friend's story, she didn't believe it because she was too sad to accept it! Had she welcomed this awesome supernatural news, the husband's soul would have continued to try to get her attention—but she didn't, so he put his signs on hold. It wasn't until I read the wife that she became open to Spirit communication, and his soul said he'd give it another shot. "A cold chill, warmth, a shadow, a song on the radio—that's your husband," I said. "It's his way of reaching out."

Signs can arrive when you desperately need them or as a surprise, but I've come to believe that the higher your expectations, the harder it is to sense Spirit. I'm not sure if this is a universal energy dynamic or plain ol' human nature. It's like what happens when you tear the house apart looking for a lost ring, and it's been under your nose all along. Given that signs tend to be subtle, there's a good chance that while you were desperately waiting for an apparition, Grandma sent you a beautiful message in a song or floated a feather right onto your daughter's head. Be open too to different interpretations—this is no time to split hairs or become a literalist. For instance, if you can connect with ladybugs, accept the living ones that randomly crawl up your kitchen wall as well as those that appear on purses or the dish towel at your friend's house. Eliminating strict expectations about what a soul should send gives Spirit greater freedom about how they associate with you. Now, I'm not saying you need to accept *any* random occurrence as a sign, but don't close yourself off from a huge blessing by being nitpicky. Spirit doesn't always send signs that exactly match our thoughts or memories, but they're usually in the ballpark.

A sign's timing is significant in determining its meaning too. My client Summer, whose story I shared in chapter 11, received a special sign from her daughter Season when the family went to dinner to honor the second anniversary of the infant's departure. "At one point during the meal, I quietly asked Season's soul to be near me, and as we were leaving, I sat down in the lobby, which was very dark," Summer said. "I looked down into the windowsill and saw a brand-new—with tags still attached—golden ring wedged into a crack. The black packaging was facing outward, so it was almost impossible to see, but I felt I just had to reach my hand down into the windowsill." The object was a little crown, and Summer just knew it was from her daughter. "There was no question I was meant to find it." The shiny, dime-store trinket now sits on top of a pink quartz angel, against a backdrop of lace, next to Season's ashes. "It was a Heavenly gift from my angel girl," she says, "whose room and colors have always been pink and gold."

Bottom line, Spirit does their part by showing up in amazing ways. Your job is to be open to what's going on around you and embrace their signs, knowing that these are from your loved ones.

Learn Spirit's Sign Language

Spirit communicates with us through signs and symbols, some of the more typical being random feathers, loose change, animals, songs, insects, license plate messages, number sequences like 111, meaningful times on the clock, and religious articles. When you mentally establish that the soul sends daisies or the smell of cologne, they will continue to do this. (You can agree on a sign for the person to send *before* they pass, but this isn't necessary and doesn't always work.) As you now know, Spirit is not literally the object, or even in the object; they're using their energy to move, interact with, or direct your attention to these things. Spirit can also prompt you to turn on the radio or look at the clock at a significant time. They might even direct your attention to someone who looks similar to how they did in this world. One of my favorite types of signs is when Spirit uses their energy to touch your body or wrap their soul around you so that you feel chills or a warm, tingly energy. It's similar to how they can energetically envelop an object like a rocking chair to make it move or solidify it next to you to make an impression on the bed.

Spirit's an ace at finagling items in your home as well. They tilt pictures, move objects, turn the volume up on your TV, make items go missing, and cause your pets to freak out. It's easy for them to fuss with electrical equipment—lamps, TVs, kids' toys—because they're made of energy too. They can also cause the sound of knocking, footsteps, or dishes clanging around in the kitchen. All of this requires a lot of energy, so they're working very hard to get you to notice them if this is happening to you!

And though real-life visuals like apparitions or faces in your bathroom mirror are rare, Spirit isn't shy about showing off their energy in photos as a blue haze, orb, streak, or white, smoky cloud that *I* can't even sense until I look at the image. And sometimes if you zoom in on an orb, you can see a face! Souls can appear as people too—usually as a hologram or obscured in an orb or cloud. When this happens, I compare it to how a dog can hear a super-high pitch but we can't. A lot of electronic equipment, like a camera or phone, is the same way— it can pick up on frequencies that we don't. If you look back at photos of your own celebrations or family gatherings, you may see an orb or image that surprises you.

Because I love music, I have a special affinity for lyrical signs. This reminds me of a reading I did at a live show in Fargo, North Dakota. Here, Spirit led me to a woman named Codi whose son Eli died when he was one and a half years old. Eli, along with his twin brother Trey, were at their father's house for the weekend. The day he passed, his father's friend was watching the boys and her son. She'd just run the water for Eli, when she heard one of the other boys crying. She told Eli to sit tight, next to the tub, and wait for her. When she returned only three and a half minutes later, Eli had drowned.

Since Eli died, Codi has felt her son's soul around her and while all of his signs lift her heart, musical ones really strike a chord. "There are many, many times when I'm feeling down and need to feel my son," she says, "and then all of a sudden, a song will come on the radio from Eli's funeral or remind me of him—mostly 'Watching You' by Rodney Atkins or 'Angel' by Sarah McLachlan." She also associates "You Are My Sunshine" with Eli, because "it's the first song I sang to them as babies and then again, when I held Eli alone in the ER after the drowning. Once they pronounced him dead, they wrapped him in warm blankets, dimmed the lights, and let me be alone in the room with him. I kissed him over and over as I sang to him and begged him to wake up." When Codi hears any of Eli's songs, she can't help but shake her head, smile, look to the sky, and whisper, "I love you too, sweetheart."

Making the Connection

We all connect with Spirit in our own, natural way. Some clients see signs, while others feel a soul's presence or tune into sound. This is why a wife can see a figure at the foot of the bed, but her husband, lying next to her, can't see a thing. Or why a sister dreams of her dead parents, but her brother sees two baby frogs on his porch instead; the parents' souls use their energy in ways to which their kids are most receptive. Spirit says to stay open to different pathways until you know how *you* connect best.

You can ask for a sign from Spirit if you need encouragement, but loved ones can sense this on their own. I read a woman named Pam and her husband, Rolando, at a live show in Orlando, Florida; they lost their twenty-nine-year-old son, Anthony, to a brain tumor. Pam says that she receives countless signs from Anthony, mostly through feelings and objects placed in her path. For instance, hanging on his bedroom wall is a photo of Anthony during his last fishing trip with his dad; every evening, Pam tells him "Good night" and how much she loves and misses him. As she does this, she said she can feel Anthony's soul beside her—and during her reading, Anthony's soul validated that he hears his mom's words and is with her as well. Pam also connects with her son through butterflies. Once, she was feeling a little blue while shopping and looked down to see a purple silk butterfly on the ground and picked it up. Then, three days later, she was about to enter a different store and saw *another* silk butterfly on the ground—this one was purple and blue! Purple is Pam's favorite color, and her son had beautiful blue eyes. Unless there was some kind of weird silk insect convention going on, there's no way this was anything *but* Spirit!

When you get a sign from a loved one, say hi, tell the soul you miss them, fill them in on any news from your life, or just say "I love you." You don't need to have a long conversation. Acknowledging Spirit's presence is enough. And don't feel bad if you've been too distracted to connect! Just say to Spirit, "If I don't talk to you as much today or miss your signs, I still love and miss you."

The More Things Change

Over time, you'll notice that by embracing signs, your soul will undergo a more complete healing and growth process. You'll no longer question where your loved one is, if they know what's going on in your life or what's in store for your own soul when you die. You'll also help Spirit communicate more readily and fluidly because you'll no longer second-guess what you're shown—and this encourages them to send more signs and guide you in different ways. You'll integrate signs, and Spirit, into your day in a healthy way, because you'll accept and really appreciate their ability to love and protect you.

Know too that a soul's energy and abilities will advance as the soul grows and heals on the Other Side. This allows Spirit to communicate differently and often better. Signs, then, get an update. So now, maybe you won't see lights flicker, but you may hear the soul's voice in your mind or talk to each other in dreams. It reminds me of how when Gram first died, the woman surrounded us with dimes. Victoria would sit on a dime at her gymnastics meets, and at Gramps's wake, we noticed a dime under her seat. Then at a live show in Westbury, Long Island, a dime just appeared on the stage and rolled in front of me when I was giving my opening speech! I don't think my dry-cleaner's cutting holes in my family's pockets . . . ? And while I still find the random dime, Gram's lately advanced to manipulating my iPhone. One day, a crazy rap song began playing on my phone, and a week later, I found Michael Bublé's "Try a Little Tenderness" on there, and I never downloaded it. I have to assume Gram is behind both, though I didn't know she had such diverse tastes! Who knows? Maybe she's hanging with Tupac in Heaven.

Healing Moments

This week, stay extra aware of Spirit's presence using all of your senses. In your journal, write down all the signs you receive and what you interpret each one to mean. Simply by reading this chapter, Spirit becomes aware of your intentions to embrace their hellos, so enjoy them. Also, try to remember the way it feels to notice and accept a sign—maybe a quick, subtle inclination to notice, turn, or move in the direction of a sign, before or after thinking of a loved one—so that you're aware of it for future reference!

14

Coincidence, Shmo-incidence

I like to talk about coincidences separate from other signs, because I think they're so freaking special. While Spirit mostly speaks to us through subtleties like symbols and whispers in your gut, coincidences are about as loud as your loved ones can get. With each one, Spirit might as well be saying, "BOOYA! Did you see what I just did there?!" Coincidences grab your attention right away, since you don't have to interpret them to experience their impact. Their face value is extraordinary enough. And while you can make all the excuses you want for why you see signs like a dragonfly on your therapist's window or the same rabbit every day in your yard, there's no doubting when a coincidence happens. What takes faith is accepting that they're undeniably sent by Spirit to enhance your happiness, well-being, inner peace, and overall serenity. Your loved ones have a vested interest in scenarios that might impact those feelings.

What's in a Coincidence?

The first thing you need to know about a coincidence is that there's no such thing as a coincidence! If a situation feels coincidental, it's happening for a reason—and the primary reason is that Spirit's moving the chess pieces to create a situation that grabs your attention and will somehow improve your life, whether it's to make you smile, feel reassured or comforted, keep you safe, or make your day a little easier. (Another term for an intentional coincidence is "synchronicity," which is when two or more events that seem unrelated come together in a meaningful way . . . but I'm going to just use the word "coincidence" here, because we can all relate to it.) As you grieve, some examples of coincidences might include overhearing a conversation that validates what you're feeling, hitting all the green lights so you can get to your support group on time, finding out shortly after your husband dies that an old friend is moving back to town after her husband recently passed too—those kinds of things. And though you might feel like you spend a lot of time feeling sad, Spirit doesn't only arrange coincidences related to your grief. Spirit gives you what you need, in any area of your life, so long as it is meaningful to you at that time.

Spirit tells me there's a second reason coincidences exist, which is to teach you how to become more in tune with your intuition and better judgment. They encourage you to admit that you're connected to something much bigger than yourself. When a coincidence occurs, you might not realize it, but you have to respond to an instinctual nudge to think about or do something and then participate in how the coincidence comes together. Like if you wonder if your son's plane landed safely and then seconds later look at your phone to see that a text from him says it did, or if you feel blue and think a walk might help so you head outside and bump into a friend who tells you a funny story, your instincts are at play here.

Let's break down how a coincidence works. So, say you're thinking of your mom and she calls a second later—that's so weird, what just happened? Well first, Spirit—often a loved one, but maybe an angel or guide—sees, hears, or feels your need to connect with Mom since it's Spirit's job to love, guide, and protect you; don't ask me how

Spirit senses this, but I'm shown that it involves their energy connecting with your energy field, and that's all I know. Then Spirit prompts Mom's intuition to call not just at any time, but at a time that will feel meaningful to you—the moment you think of her, at a time when you're upset, whatever the case may be. Now I'm not saying that Spirit has its eyes on you all day, spying on you during a shower or when you sneak an Oreo from the cookie jar. But they are always sensing when you need assistance and devising opportunities for you to either act on or ignore using your free will. Finally, coincidences occur when you don't expect them, so the fact that you didn't ask God for Mom to call is key. It's why, no matter how often coincidences happen, they always feel surprising!

A coincidence's timing is very important, because it must occur at a juncture that makes an impact either by speaking to your needs at that moment or impressing you with the feeling that *you've been heard*. This reminds me of how, on the anniversary of Gramps's death, I was thinking that I couldn't believe it had been two years since he was reunited with Gram in Heaven. A few minutes later, I hopped into my car to go to the gym, and I turned on the radio. It was 9:10 a.m.—and my grandfather died shortly after nine a.m. What song do you think comes on? "After the Lovin' " by Engelbert Humperdinck, which is the song that I always remember Gram and Gramps dancing to at my wedding! *And the love on your face / is so real that it makes me want to cry* . . . It's not like that song is usually playing at all, much less when I happen to be in the car, thinking about my grandparents! Without a doubt, I knew this coincidence was their way of telling me they were dancing together in Heaven. It was intended to make me smile.

Though you don't want to overthink the purpose of a coincidence, it is nice to acknowledge that they happen for a reason, if just so you recognize all the incredible ways that Spirit supports you. Sometimes a coincidence is a validation that you're on the right track in life or made the right choice—especially if your decision is intuition-based. Larry gets a kick out of coincidences when he notices how his gut matches up with real life—he'll be thinking about his T-shirt line and then come across some awesome inspiration the next day, or wonder about a friend he hasn't seen in ages and then bump into him at the tattoo parlor. Larry jokes that this is *my* ESP rubbing off on him, but I actually think he's just become more aware and accepting of how Spirit works through his own intuition and finds it amazing.

Coincidences serve functional purposes too, like when Spirit sends you opportunities and offers guidance. If we ask for help during meditation or prayer, or if Spirit senses you need a hand, they may present you with a coincidental opportunity or send you a coincidental sign that validates that they're aware of the choices and decisions you have to make. For instance, if you're thinking about adopting a dog to help raise your mood, Spirit might arrange a coincidence where you either "happen to hear" about a friend whose dog needs a new home or flip on the TV to see Sarah McLaughlin's heartbreaking ASPCA commercial, which prompts you to visit a local shelter. The dog you decide to get is up to you, however, because Spirit doesn't make choices for you. At most, they'll intervene if you're headed down the wrong path by sending you coincidental opportunities to steer you back! Coincidences aren't to be ignored.

In fact, coincidences can keep you safe through instinctual warnings. It's like when you turn left instead of right and then later learn there was an accident on the alternate route; or when you decide to replenish your first-aid kit, which comes in handy when you get a bee sting the next day. I'll never forget when my friend Jenny was at brunch with her family and thought out of nowhere, *Would I know what to do if my baby choked?* She quickly but carefully thought about how she'd respond if this were to happen, then moved on to another thought. Ten minutes later, her son actually began choking on his pancakes— and because Jenny had just reviewed first-aid tips in her head, she was poised to act and knew just how to save the day. Another cool story along these safety lines is how my client Marie went to see her doctor because she had a terrible chest cold. Her symptoms were mostly gone and her doctor said she was healing, but on her way home, she still felt a little rattled. Just before her exit, Marie got stuck behind a lumbering van that was transporting medical oxygen tanks with the words "Just *breathe*" along the side. Marie laughed and immediately knew her loved ones were saying she'd be breathing fine in no time.

Divine intervention, however, doesn't have to be life or death; Spirit's on the case if they can create a scenario that makes any aspect of your life sunnier. My friend Christina, for instance, once spent an entire day mattress shopping in a fancy part of town and was bummed that her favorite choice was the most expensive. That night, she took her husband back to the store to show him anyway. On the ride there, she said, "I'll bet people with huge homes around here buy, like, five mattresses at a time to fill all their bedrooms." It was a passing thought, nothing more. At the store, the salesman was happy to see Christina. "Tonight's your lucky night!" he said. "I'm going to make a fat commission on a man who was in here just before you. He just bought a house and needed mattresses for all five bedrooms! So now I can give you a very good price." Christina couldn't believe the coincidence, and I saw that her grandmother was actually involved in orchestrating this serendipitous moment. She slept twice as nicely knowing this!

But of all coincidences, some of the most impactful are when Spirit creates scenarios that help us connect and communicate with our loved ones. I've seen Spirit move the energetic equivalent of mountains to make this happen because they need you to know they're with you. I'm thinking of how, at a live show I did in Brooklyn, a couple's daughter couldn't attend at the last minute so they sold the ticket to a lovely stranger who, of course, ended up sitting beside them. Well, that night, Spirit pulled me to this girl who, out of three thousand people, received an incredible reading! Her boyfriend had drowned in Boston Harbor while out drinking with his friends, and he wanted her to know he took responsibility for his actions, which gave her peace of mind. Think of how hard Spirit worked to bring all the pieces together—they inspired the parents to buy three tickets, created a block for the daughter to be unable to come to my show, urged the girl to then buy the ticket from this family . . . it's incredible. Spirit is always anticipating your next move, and the move after that, and the move after *that*—all to demonstrate that they care. This happened with my trainer Joe too. A week before his birthday, his father's soul came to me and said, "Wish Joe a happy birthday for me." I told the soul that his message wasn't specific enough to impress Joe, so then he said, "OK, Theresa. Mention white feathers." So the next time I saw Joe, I told him the story about me having Dad up the ante, including the feather part. Joe's jaw hit the floor. "I literally pulled tiny white feathers off my shirt with a lint roller this morning!" he said. The day after his birthday was my next session. Before we got started, I sat down on a bench, and can you believe, there was a big white feather under it? "I've owned this gym for over ten years," Joe said, "and I've *never* seen a feather here before." That's Spirit for you. Now if only Joe's dad could've gotten me out of my burpees!

Healing Moments

Designate at least a page in your journal to write about an amazing coincidence that comes your way this week. Declaring your intention to do this sends a cue to Spirit that you will be open and aware of the synchronicity they arrange. After you notice it, journal about how it made you feel to receive the coincidence and why Spirit might have sent you the one they did. Did you learn a lesson? What is it?

15

What Gets Your Goat?

Do you remember that old Sesame Street cartoon about the goat that got angry all the time? He'd sing, "I get mad, I get mad, I get mad . . . it ain't bad to get meh-heh-heh-heh-aaad." Well, I'm with the garbling goat here—it's OK to freak out when you have a legitimate reason to be upset. And while grief invites a lot of anger that swings between the sensible and illogical, what matters is that it feels valid to you.

So tell me, who are you pissed at today? Is it the person who died? God? Maybe yourself? How about family members who don't seem to be grieving hard enough or friends who don't know what to say? Or what about siblings who made choices related to the person's passing or burial that you didn't agree with? Don't forget about the stupid doctors, careless nurses . . . oh, and those random, smiling strangers on the street! Listen, it's important to feel what you feel, but your list of targets—and your ongoing fury—can become endless if you don't make a conscious effort to, well, end it.

Like the goat says, it ain't bad to get mad. But you can't hold on to this feeling forever.

Anger Isn't Just About You

Though your anger may feel warranted, it's not a self-contained emotion and has far-reaching consequences for those around you. A lot of clients think, *Who cares if I'm angry? This is about me. It's nobody's business if I'm this way.* And that's true—to a point. The problem is, anger can fester and spread, becoming uncontrollable and unwieldy. It's a negative intention that can provoke really hurtful behavior. It makes you less present and can cause you to lash out and say stuff you'll regret. You might ignore a friend or snap at a child who needs you because all you see is your own rage. You might even cause irreversible harm to another person who turns around to hurt you! I remember reading a man who lost his sibling in a fight, and he kept saying, "If I ever find who did this, look out. I'm going to seriously hurt him." He was out to get an eye for an eye. But the brother's soul told him to stop the anger because it would cause him to commit a crime he'd regret—and that single reaction could change his life forever.

The thing about anger is that you may feel like it has a grip on you, but Spirit says that you actually hold on to anger. The more you choose to focus on anger, the less you pay attention to the guilt, fear, longing, or other sticky emotions at its source. During the grief process, anger is the perfect distraction from what's really upsetting you. If you focus on the fact that your late sister's ex didn't take her to the doctor enough, then you don't have to pay attention to the fact that you miss her desperately. Refusing to let go of your anger might also make you feel like you're holding on to your loved one, because their passing provoked this rawness in you. More than anything else, though, Spirit says we latch on to anger because it gives us a false sense of control—instead of feeling defenseless, we use anger to exert our influence over our world and everyone else's lives. Yet while it gives you back a sense of power, the rush is fleeting. In the long run, anger will deplete you and your relationships. It will chip at your soul. And if you turn your anger on yourself, there's a good chance you'll fall into a depression or resort to self-destructive behaviors like overeating or drinking a nightly bottle of pinot noir to feel better.

Anger Doesn't Fly Solo

Anger is not a simple emotion that exists in isolation. If you allow anger to dominate your life, other negative feelings will follow. Panic, sadness, hurt, loneliness, and blame are gonna sneak up right behind it. You might not even realize that these emotions are offshoots of anger, because your feelings aren't simple or one-dimensional; they're complicated, messy, and hard to pull apart sometimes. It's like with the woman I once read who lost her little sister in a car accident. When I channeled the girl's soul, she said, "Please tell my sister not to be angry." As if on cue, the woman yelled, "*I'M* NOT ANGRY?!" To which the sister's soul said, "You're upset that I didn't ask you for a ride that night." So, at first blush, it might have seemed to the woman that she didn't feel anger, because she may have called it regret or guilt. But these are anger's deceptive cohorts. It can be hard to tell when all these negative feelings are related.

Blame is an especially dangerous one-off from anger because it actually feels good to let it rip! Plus, when you're irate, your instinct is to move as far away from that feeling as you can because it hurts—even if that means pushing it into someone else's lap. Since blame finds fault, often where there is none, it offers the perfect solution to basically every question and struggle you have. I mean, if you say that a death is an ex's or oncologist's fault, you know exactly where to funnel your anger—toward that person—and then *you* have less to deal with. Blame is a terrific emotional release that way.

I can't say I'm surprised when clients blame God for "letting a person suffer" or "causing a death." When I'm mad as can be, you better believe I want to take it out on someone else (usually Larry or one of the kids!). And let's face it—it's cathartic to hoot and holler at an invisible energy, right? God's been rumored to burn a bush or two, but it's not like you have to worry about watching Him express hurt when you yell at Him or hurl insults right back at you in a booming voice!

The key to avoiding the temptation of blame is to realize that God doesn't "let people suffer," cause death, or snatch souls away from family and friends. Yes, God originally created your soul from His energy. But with each incarnation, your destiny window is determined by your guides and your own soul. Spirit says this timeline is based on how long it will take you to learn the lessons you need to absorb plus influence the lessons of others. Though it's not always this way, I have noticed that a lot of people who die young, particularly kids, have mature souls and, therefore, fewer lessons to pursue. I believe they pack a lifetime of happiness, wisdom, and goodwill into a short period because their souls know they signed on for a brief journey.

So many of my clients assume that if they're generally good people, faithful to God, and/or pray a lot, then bad things won't happen to them or other good people for that matter. And when this assumption proves to be untrue, they become livid. I can relate to this too, because when Gram passed from what felt like an incredibly unfair situation, I was more than ready to rail at God. After suffering a miscarriage as a young woman, Gram contracted hepatitis C from a blood transfusion but was misdiagnosed with hepatitis B and treated accordingly. When she was correctly diagnosed fifteen years later, she couldn't make up for the lost time and was eventually told she had cirrhosis of the liver from the original infection. Do you think I never felt, *Why Gram, God? How could you do this to her?* Gram was the most faithful, kind, compassionate, and loving person I've ever known. Never complained a day in her life. But every time I'd start to get mad at the universe over her disease, a voice inside would remind me that if Gram hadn't had the transfusion, we wouldn't have been able to enjoy her until the ripe age of eighty-five! In fact, between the transfusion and her passing, she also overcame breast cancer, a melanoma on her nose, and scarring in her lungs from the cirrhosis and Gramps's secondhand smoke! So I had to make peace with the fact that what ultimately gave Gram a longer, stronger life is also what caused her passing—and more important, that her trials taught her tolerance that ultimately grew her soul.

The good news is that when I channel God, He always says that if you need to blame Him to feel better, it's OK. You can be as angry at God as you want, but He will never stop loving and guiding you from Heaven. It's like how during a live show in Columbus, Ohio, I read a woman named Dawn who lost her eighteen-year-old daughter Jessica in a car accident. She spent months praying to God and her daughter's soul to come through at the show, and Jessica's was the first I channeled! When Jessica initially died, Dawn was understandably angry—for the first few months, she'd scream, cry, and pound on the steering wheel of her car or yell Jessica's name in the house, hoping she'd somehow answer. The experience was so painful that Dawn, an otherwise spiritual person, began to doubt whether she believed in God or an afterlife at all: *What kind of loving God would let this kind of thing happen? Why take my daughter? Why not me?*

Yet after our reading, Dawn felt wholly reassured that Jessica's soul lives on—the fact that I could channel her was all the proof she needed to know she's not gone forever. "That my daughter came through proved to me that I must have faith," she said. "I felt an overwhelming comfort and acknowledgment that God and Heaven are real." Now Dawn talks to God and her daughter's soul every day while sitting on a bench made in Jessica's memory, and believes God helped me deliver the exact messages that would reinforce her beliefs and soothe her rage. After the show, Dawn and her husband, in fact, dedicated themselves to a better relationship with God. Now they go to church and appreciate His gifts to humanity, especially in nature—"a twinkle of the stars, the clouds in the sky, the beautiful animals in our woods, and the flowers in our yard," she said. Dawn also prays, rather than yells, in the car whenever "the mood strikes." She wears a cross and ring containing Jessica's ashes every day. "I'm still working on my relationship with God, but my heart is so much fuller when I feel the love that I get from my faith," she adds. To feel close to God is to feel close to where her daughter's soul dwells.

I want to be honest and note that Dawn's renewed faith hasn't miraculously removed every last ounce of her anger, but it's helped heal a large corner of it, and that's still tremendous since healing and clarity happen in moments and increments. In fact, Dawn lately finds herself feeling disappointed with many of Jessica's friends from school who seemed to have forgotten about her. Rather than privately fume, she knows it's better to pour her frustration into something good. She created a Facebook memory page, talks about Jessica in a parent grief group, and got a tattoo on her forearm to keep Jessica's memory alive. "These things help me feel better, because I do them to honor my beautiful daughter," she said. Beating back her indignation with positive gestures, a little at a time, has been really helpful to her.

Feeling Trigger-Happy?

Because anger is the front man for a band of negative feelings stemming from grief, it sure would be nice to know what sets you off so you can avoid these triggers, but the truth is, they're pretty unpredictable! Anger's catalysts also change as you do. The good news is that when a trigger provokes anger, it's helpful to feel it, move through it, and then put it to rest to see that it's not worth how sick it makes you. If you do this enough times, you'll feel ready to turn the page. In that way, at least anger is useful.

Remember my client Clara, whom I mentioned in chapter 2, who lost her husband, Jo, to a heart attack? She says that her anger was fierce and deep for a long time, and that it didn't take much to set her off. "I was angry at everyone," she said. "God mostly, but almost everyone else in my life too. I hated people who were too happy; I hated people who were too sad—I thought I reserved the right to be the saddest. I hated people who were having babies. I hated being with friends who complained about nonsense. These feelings were around for three years before I saw a shift, but I worked really hard to shift my attitude. It didn't just happen. I had better periods and much worse periods, but the anger was always with me. I was just so, so sad." What I appreciate about Clara's anger is that it helped her feel her honest feelings to the nth degree, which is what it took to figure out what would help her keep going—including a new job, apologizing to friends she treated unfairly, and freezing her eggs for future babies. Five years after Jo's death, Clara still goes to bed every night thinking about her husband, but while his absence is with her all the time, it doesn't consume every second of her day like it did. "I'm still really upset that he's gone obviously, but I'm now more grateful for the time we had together," she said. "I'm happy we loved each other, and I am really positive that his soul is with me. I know I'll see him again one day."

All that being said, if another person *does* carelessly feed your anger—like your mom's boss who asks why your brother committed suicide or your friend who hears you've miscarried and says, "I'm a little *too* fertile! You can have one of mine!"—to them, I say, *zip it*. You don't owe anyone an explanation, and you don't need to engage. Unless, of course, it makes you feel better to say your piece. At the end of the goat ditty on *Sesame Street*, the song concludes, *"And in the end, most folks are glad / to find out what makes him mad . . ."* So if you tell people they're being insensitive, it may help you both.

Healing Moments

The next time you're pissed off, Spirit says to try a grounding exercise to send your negative emotions deep into the earth. First, in the space below, I want you to list the top three reasons why you feel angry right now—not when the person first died, not a week ago, but at the very moment you're seething. Then sit in a meditation pose and imagine using your energy to push all the negative feelings you've attached to those reasons into the ground, and envision this murky gray energy swirling beneath you and turning back into twinkly white light. Push this divine light up and into your body, filling yourself with it. Give yourself a hug, and don't let go until you're ready. Now look at your list again and notice how the anger you held in your body feels a little farther away. Draw a big **X** through your list and turn the page!

16

Let Your Anger Loose

Yes, it's vital to admit and feel your anger, but you can't stop there. You must *release* it in a way that doesn't hurt you or others. At some point, you'll need to ask yourself, *Haven't I had enough of this outrage? Of the infuriating loop that plays over and over in my head? Of the exasperation that kills my will to participate in life?* Hiding under all that indignation is pain, and nothing good comes from suppressing or holding on to either one. The longer you ignore what this negativity does to you, the more it dominates your days and relationships. The way anger affects you is like how a marshmallow behaves in the microwave. It bubbles and swells until it's forced to collapse into a sticky, unrecognizable mess!

It's no big surprise that Spirit says you choose how to handle your aggression. So if you need to muck around in a dark place for a little longer, I can't stop you. But please do this knowing it's not what your loved ones want and that the only way anger can fully serve you—now that you've really felt and lived it—is if you let it go. During a reading, Spirit often says, "I need you to love and honor yourself, your life, and your family more than the anger you carry connected with my departure." In other words, embrace what's happening around you, rather than the searing internal monologue that's eating you alive.

Talk It Out

Most of my clients' go-to mechanism for releasing anger is verbalizing it. Telling a counselor, family member, a friend you trust, or even yourself how you feel unloads a lot of negativity from your soul. Don't hold back either—yell and cry with everything you've got. Or, if you're feeling self-conscious, write about your feelings in your journal. And while Spirit says that going full throttle in one sitting might be plenty cathartic, it's OK if you need to vent more often. Be true to your bottomless pit of rage. The goal is to unpack as many angry feelings as you can, and to whomever you need, to finally feel free.

If your anger is justified, you may want to consider confronting the person who's upset you. Just be sure, however, to adjust your expectations based on the other person's limits. For instance, if you're furious at the orderlies for how you feel they cared for your late father, and your sister doesn't agree with your opinion, lay out how you feel. Be specific about what bothered you, and why—really spell out the details—so that nothing is missed or misunderstood. Stay away from blame and be sure to (1) make your goal a mutual understanding and recognition of how *everyone* feels, and (2) adjust your expectations according to what the other person is capable of feeling, saying, or doing in response. So if your sister has a tendency to avoid confrontation and bow to authority, don't expect her to suggest a meeting with the hospital's board of directors. A friend once said to me, if a person is missing a leg, you wouldn't expect her to kick you a ball. It's a nice metaphor to keep in mind when you're in any kind of conflict.

Spirit also says that you can yell at your deceased loved ones all you want—and while they might call you out in a reading, Spirit never gets offended! Bottom line, they want you to do whatever you need to heal, and if that means shouting at the sky or screaming at their photo, have at it. I know Spirit can hear you because they always mention it in a funny way when I channel them. I remember reading a woman who, every day, yelled at her husband's soul for leaving her, and when he came through, he jokingly said, "Tell my wife to stop shouting at me!" Or how about when I channeled a man who was furious over his brother's death? His soul said to me, "Theresa, he yelled at me when they closed the casket! You tell him, 'F*ck you too!'" This cracked us up, because sure enough, the brother said, "I did say that to him! He heard me?" Look, Spirit knows why you'd behave this way, but validating it like this gets you to laugh. I think it's a clever tactic on Spirit's part, because levity breaks up your tension and lightens your vibration. Then, when Spirit asks you to release your anger, you're that much closer to accepting their advice.

And by the way, when you're done with your bellyaching, you can always ask for Spirit's help. Just say out loud or in your head, "Please guide me out of this anger or show me outlets to see things differently." You can direct the request toward your loved ones or any divine soul on the Other Side that you trust, including God of course. Be patient as you wait for these opportunities to surface, whether it's meeting a new friend who's a great listener or just talking to a stranger who asks how you're feeling, just when you're about to explode. I know you're already pissed, but try not to be anxious about when these moments will happen. Spirit always says, "Just because your prayers aren't answered right away doesn't mean God isn't paying attention to you." Sometimes you have to be patient for His gifts to arrive.

Do Something

Doing a physical activity lets you channel your energy into an actionable task. Remember, your mind, body, and soul are connected, so engaging your body will affect your mind and soul too. How you decide to move is up to you. I've heard great stories about spinning marathons and punching pillows, but the more creative and personal you can make this, the more effective it will be at offering you a release.

Choose an activity that helps you shed your anger, either by mentally separating you from it or reinforcing other types of healing bonds. I'm a big fan of detoxifying the body, and I always find it cathartic to sweat like crazy in a sauna for twenty minutes. There's nothing a good *shvitz* can't help! After all, saunas are proven to reduce stress, relax muscles, yield deeper sleep, and improve your immune system among other benefits—all important factors that help you heal. You can even close your eyes and visualize that your pores are excreting all negativity like resentment and sorrow. Another great activity for grief and anger is equine therapy, since horses are naturally social animals that form strong bonds with their riders. They're very sensitive creatures that mirror your feelings, and a lot of grievers experience an uplifting effect, emotional release, and a new sense of pride that replaces the hostility and loneliness that brings them down. An equine therapist can also watch how you interact with a fine filly or stallion, and then shed light on specific emotional issues you may need to work through to help you fully heal.

What's most significant is to make the emotional release your own. I heard a great story about a woman named Jenn who, along with her sisters, have a consistent practice for when they're angry over a loss. They shatter dishes! After both sets of Jenn's grandparents died, the sisters rented a metal dumpster and threw old, worthless plates against the inside of it. "We call it 'playing Frisbee,' " she said. And when Jenn's mom suddenly passed from a heart attack, the women didn't want to ruin anything of sentimental value so they hit Goodwill to stock up on someone else's old tableware. Back at Mom's house, they strapped on safety goggles and smashed plates on the driveway pavement to get out their anger. Even the aftermath was cleansing.

"Quietly sweeping up the pieces, after creating such chaos, gave us a chance to catch our breath and reflect on how we felt," she said. "It was more Zen than you'd think!"

Lend a Helping Hand

Finally, a lot of my clients feel an enormous relief when they funnel their anger into positive gestures for others. Of all three options, this has the most powerful effect because it literally transforms negative into positive energy—and Spirit knows that takes a lot of strength. As you think about how to serve others, begin with intentions that are good and pure. If your motivations are misdirected or inappropriate, Spirit says it won't release your rage long term or heal your soul. So as an example, let's say your spouse dies from myocarditis related to Lyme disease, which you feel is an under-researched and underfunded condition. Your anger would be better channeled into working with a foundation that funds great education and research that speaks for itself rather than writing nasty articles that take down the institutions, doctors, and guidelines you hate. I'm not saying your venom wouldn't be warranted or appease a certain audience. But if your goal is to eradicate the anger and heal your soul, looking back and fixing blame isn't how you do it. Your energy could even tip into something martyred, vindictive, and almost bullying. Using anger to promote good, rather than feed more anger, is what turns the tables on negativity.

I have a number of clients who pay it forward to make a loved one's soul proud, and in turn help a lot of people. This is like my client Ashley, who was just ten years old when she lost her uncle Jerry, a father figure to her. In fact, when I channeled Jerry's soul, he called her "the daughter I never had." Though it's been many years since he passed, Ashley is still furious about how her uncle died, since she feels it could have been prevented. As it happened, Jerry fractured his hip and was bedridden in the hospital while waiting for hip replacement surgery. Because he wasn't moving around, Ashley said the staff should have put compression socks on Jerry's legs to encourage blood flow—yet because they didn't, a clot formed and rushed to Jerry's lungs. He died instantly. When I channeled Uncle Jerry's soul, he said to Ashley, "Follow your dreams and make a difference," and Ashley took those words to heart. "I was angry then, and I still get angry now," she said, "but I want to make my uncle proud." To that end, Ashley has become a volunteer EMT plus a nursing student who works in the emergency department. "Every time I step foot in the hospital or ambulance, I do this with my uncle in mind and to prevent what happened to him from happening to another," she said. "I don't want anyone else to experience the senseless loss that I have."

Others put their anger aside to do good in a way that reflects their loved one's interests. At a show in Westbury, New York, I read a woman named Kristina whose thirteen-year-old son Trent died in a UTV accident. I channeled his soul just two months after he passed. Trent and five other kids, including his sister, spent the day at a birthday party where they rode around on the vehicle at a responsible speed while wearing seat belts. On Trent's way back from his last venture out, just as the kids pulled up to the house, the vehicle flipped over for an unknown reason. And while the other passengers experienced minor if any injuries, the vehicle landed directly on Trent's head and killed him. The hospital, in fact, told Trent's family that it was the worst head trauma they'd ever witnessed. "And to think that earlier that day," said Kristina, "I'd even thought to myself, 'This has been such a perfect day.' "

When I read Kristina, she told me she was managing her anger as best she could. She can't let go of others' comments about God, though. "What makes me the angriest is when people say God wanted Trent to come home," she said. "I believe in God, but not that He would just randomly pluck a soul from earth, as if he were bored and had nothing better to do." She also gets upset with herself for things she didn't say to her son and requests he'd made that she didn't give in to—little stuff, mostly. "I wish we'd been more patient with him, told him more often that we were proud of him, and were more spontaneous about spending fifteen minutes in the park enjoying each other's company or stopped what we were doing to play a game he wanted," she said. "It all comes to you after it's too late and you don't get do-overs."

Even so, I'll be honest: Kristina's outlets for anger are among the most inspiring I've seen. "Trent was always looking out or sticking up for others, so we do a lot of random acts of kindness that will make a difference in other people's lives and at the same time honor Trent's memory," she said. "It also keeps us busy and motivated to do good things." When Trent died and donations were sent to her family, they forwarded the money to a local shelter because Trent was a huge animal lover; they take up donations on the anniversary of Trent's death and send them here too. For Christmas, Kristina's family adopts a family in need and provides them with clothes, shoes, coats, and toys. They also buy gifts for patients at Cincinnati Children's Hospital, where Trent was treated. Perhaps sweetest of all, Kristina passes out business cards with Trent's adorable, cheesing picture on it—on the front of the card it says, "Random Acts of Kindness in Memory of Trent Myers," and on the back, "Please enjoy this random act of kindness in honor of our loved one. Our hope is that you will perform an act of kindness as well and pass this card on." So far, Kristina's mostly given these out while paying for the car behind her in a drive-through and at restaurants. She's left an extralarge tip for the waitress with the card, plus coins in the game machines at the movie theater or mall. And on Trent's birthday, she left gift cards with cashiers at two grocery stores and also at Gamestop, Trent's favorite video game and electronics store. Is that awesome or what?

Healing Moments

Let's release some anger! Maybe you can't get past how furious you feel toward your departed brother-in-law for not remembering you in his will or your deceased ex-husband for cheating on you years ago. Even if you're on your way to healing, I'll bet you have a lingering grievance that begs to be set free. No matter what the injustice, it's time to let the situation go—*for good*—and try not to revisit it. Think about what will satisfy you the most—your soul knows the answer. Gentle confrontation? Banging on a drum? Writing furiously about the situation, and then ripping up the paper and throwing it away? Go for it!

17

Getting Past the Past

Your departed loved ones talk a lot about the shoulda/woulda/coulda/if onlys connected to a passing. I have a sneaking suspicion that you know what I mean by this.

I should have been a better wife.

I could have been a more patient caretaker.

I would have picked him up from the party had I known he was drinking.

If only we'd caught the cancer sooner.

And how do you imagine Spirit reacts when they hear these thoughts? "You're right, you insensitive son of a *bleep*"? Of course not! They implore you to stop going over the past and to release all burdens, guilt, and regrets related to their passing. They say what's done is done—their destiny was set long ago, and you couldn't have changed the course of things. Yet right now, you can't stop beating yourself up over the notion that you were supposed to control how and when your loved one's time here ended, and that's just not the case. This is real life, not a lost episode of *The Twilight Zone*. Harping on these imaginary scenarios won't bring anyone back; it only handcuffs you to the past and evades the truth.

Spirit says you turn to the shoulda/woulda/coulda/if onlys because it's easier to default to punishing fiction than come to grips with an actual, sad death. And while regrets and wishful thinking are natural knee-jerk reactions to loss, they don't deal in the now. Retracing your steps and reimagining the past doesn't bring you any closer to accepting what happened and then carrying on. Spirit asks you to stop the shoulda/woulda/coulda/if only talk and focus on healing your soul and rebuilding your life.

Once upon a Time . . .

In the imaginary land of shoulda/woulda/coulda/if only, we aim to rewrite history, usually by striking up a deal with the universe. Part of you knows the powers-that-be won't take you up on your offer, but it feels like a Hail Mary pass that's worth a go. If nothing else, it gives your mind a break from your gloom. I mention it here not to berate you, but to let you know you're not alone. This is a common stage of grief.

When clients play the bargaining card, they usually go right to God and try to negotiate with Him like He's a vendor at the flea market. Let me just say that God does everything He can to help you heal, but in no scenario does His relationship with us involve trading favors—about death or otherwise. God can't turn back the clock to "take you instead" or make the past a dream so you'll wake up next to your loved one. He doesn't take one person to spare another, as if there's a death quota to fill in Heaven.

You might also try bargaining with your loved ones' souls. I know a woman named Isabelle whose husband, John, died ten years after they were married. "I used to beg John's soul to come back, even though I knew this was impossible," she said. "I used to tell him that if he *did* come back, I'd be so good. I'd be grateful for all we had, I'd never act uptight or anxious, I wouldn't worry about money. I would be kinder and never yell. I'd be the perfect wife and mom. I remember lying in my hallway at night, sobbing and begging for him to come home. I knew it was an insane thing to ask, but I did it anyway." Isabelle's reaction isn't unique or insane. Your loved ones tell me that when you are in a dark place like this, they are with you in spirit. Next time, try to be aware of their energy as it surrounds you with comfort.

Spirit also asks that you not regret choices that tempt you to turn against who you are. God wants you to love yourself and stand behind any reflection of that. At a Buffalo show, I read a woman named Alissa who blamed herself for her fiancé Michael's unexpected death. She was up in the theater's balcony, yet Spirit still insisted I make my way to her in my tall heels! As it turned out, Michael died from an accidental overdose. He'd been drinking all day, and Alissa refused to let him in the house that night when he got home. He went to his mother's instead. "At some point, he took a few pain pills—my pills that I didn't even know he had," said Alissa. "Last I heard from him was a text at 12:20 a.m. saying that he loved me to death." At 3:47 p.m. the next day, his brother called to say Michael died on their mom's couch. "I couldn't stop thinking that if I had just let him in the house, this never would have happened," Alissa said. Michael's soul assured me that he made a regrettable choice within his destiny window that led to his passing, and asked Alissa to let go of the baggage she carries. Rather than focus on a past she cannot change, Michael wants her to value the strong woman she was that night and is today.

You Already Did What You Should and Could

If you worry about how much you did or didn't do for your loved one, Spirit wants you to cut yourself a break. You can only do so much, and it will never feel like enough until *you* accept that it was.

When I channel loved ones, they always reinforce that you made all the right calls and decisions—doctors, treatments, living conditions, funeral-related choices, the works—because at that time, they did feel like the right choice. I remember when Gram died, I doubted how we laid her to rest—that is, without pantyhose. I remember asking Mom why she didn't put them on her, and she said, "You don't need pantyhose in Heaven," to which my son Larry said, "Gram's going commando in Heaven?!" We were doubled over laughing, and in that ridiculous moment, I realized that stockings or no stockings, Gram would be fine with whatever made us happy. When Mom picked out Gram's outfit, she was pleased with her choice, and so it was. Plus, let's be honest, Gram's soul was already in Heaven, made of light and zipping around without a care in the world. She couldn't care less if her old body had on a pair of nude L'eggs!

A very common regret is not being able to say good-bye—whether you didn't make it to the hospital on time, weren't speaking, whatever the situation may be. But Spirit always knows when you were sitting by their bedside or racing to the hospital. They talk about how you wish you'd laid in the bed with them, closed their eyes, and whispered in their ear that it was OK to go. They know that if you weren't thousands of miles away in another country you would've been there, and they know all this because they can hear your thoughts and feel your emotions. They get it. And if you were on the outs with the person and have guilt about that, Spirit always says it's water under the bridge. What's great is that Spirit is still part of your life, so you can say good-bye on your own. You don't have to mentally return to the moment they passed, and you don't need to do this with a medium. Talk to your loved ones' souls and tell them you wish you could have said good-bye. Say what you feel and trust they're listening. You can even close your eyes and visualize the scene. In every case, Spirit says you'll feel their presence to validate they've heard you—you'll sense a tug on your heart, a warmth move through your body, or like someone is standing next to you listening. You might also receive a sign from them—have a dream, hear a song on the radio that relates to your conversation, or see a license plate that reminds you of your loved one.

There is a lesson in all this second-guessing, however, which is to reinforce how crucial it is to always make choices we feel good about standing by. Because at the end of your life, you want to feel that you did everything you could to make the most of your life. Years ago, I read a woman who had signed up for gastric bypass surgery, but the only person she told about it was her husband. She'd struggled with her weight for years and was embarrassed that she couldn't lose the pounds on her own. Sadly, the surgeon encountered complications, the woman died, and because her family didn't know about her operation, they were furious and felt robbed of the chance to say good-bye. Even so, I loved that when I channeled her, her soul didn't apologize but owned this decision and asked her family to understand her perspective.

Even if You Were Psychic, You Wouldn't Have Known!

One of the biggest regrets I hear is, "I should have known . . ." As if God gives us special powers to realize when a person's about to pass and how to stop it, but you just didn't get the memo! Look, I'm a bona fide medium, and Spirit doesn't always tell *me* when a death will precisely occur or if a person is mortally ill. I don't feel this is for us to know while we're here. It would mess with our heads and keep us from embracing life with hope and positivity. We'd hobble around with one foot in the grave.

That being said, plenty of people—myself included—*do* get fishy feelings when there's a disturbance in the Force, so to speak. You might wake up with a bad vibe on the morning of a terrible accident or have a hunch that you shouldn't let your son swim in a lake the day he tragically dies from bacterial meningitis. Looking back, then, you'll feel like you went against your better instincts, but Spirit needs you to know that's not the whole story. They show me that when this occurs, it is your soul reacting to destiny information you were told before you came—so you *are* onto something—but what you feel is the conflict it presents with your current emotions. And all of this is happening on a supra-conscious level. So instead of thinking of these valid premonitions as a missed opportunity to save a life, Spirit says to see them instead as an indication of your deep and eternal soul bond with the person who died.

One of my favorite quotes from the healing and loss experts Drs. David Kessler and Elisabeth Kübler-Ross is this: "The will to save a life is not the power to stop a death." Sit with that for a minute. *The will to save a life is not the power to stop a death.* It's so good it gives me the chills! These wise words make me think of a woman I read at a Baltimore show named Leigh; her son Thomas accidentally killed his best friend and cousin, Eddie, who was twenty-three years old at the time. "The day before Eddie died, I had an ominous feeling and begged him and my son to quit their risky behaviors," she said. "At one a.m., Eddie's father came over to tell me there'd been an incident, and my world instantly fell apart." The two men were doing donuts in Thomas's truck in an open field; they did this every week, with Thomas driving and Eddie as the passenger. As the two were cruising in circles, Eddie, without warning, took off his seat belt and sat up on the windowsill, just as Thomas hit a patch of cement. This caused the truck to tip over and onto Eddie, crushing his body. Thomas himself was injured but managed to crawl out the truck's window. He attempted, along with several friends who were watching off to the side and came running, to lift the vehicle off Eddie. But when the police and EMS arrived, they pronounced Eddie dead on the scene. Just after, when Leigh saw her son at the State Police Barracks where he was held for questioning, she said Thomas was a "shadow of his former self—lifeless, as if his soul left with Eddie's."

Following the accident, Leigh said Thomas was overcome with guilt and grief—his will to live was dwindling. "I truly felt that I was in a fight to save my son's life," she said. Leigh too felt culpable because she thought she could or should have done more to stop the tragedy.

"I felt guilty for not stressing my feelings, but I came to remind myself that as an adult, Thomas had the freedom to make his own choices, as hard as it is to accept," she said. The best Leigh realized she could do, then, was to look ahead and focus on their recovery. She prayed every night that her son heal and that he'd be able to connect with Eddie via a reading with me. When I did, in fact, channel him at the show, Eddie's soul helped lift Thomas's shame by letting him know it was his "time to go that night." Eddie also revealed that Thomas bargained hard and often, praying for God to take his soul in exchange for Eddie's return, which not even Leigh knew, and then asked him to please stop torturing himself this way. At the end of the reading, Spirit said to Leigh, "Your prayers have been answered. You got your son back today." As Leigh told me later, "That night did begin Thomas's healing process and vastly improved mine. Now when I look at him, I see a purpose to live that he'd otherwise surrendered. I hear a laugh that has genuine emotion. I see a smile that warms my heart." Though Thomas knows Eddie's death wasn't his fault, Spirit says the way he passed was a choice and there are lessons in the situation that unfolded. Perhaps Leigh didn't sense just Eddie's impending death, but the lessons their souls were about to absorb from the loss.

When Fate Flips a Coin

If a client bargains, second-guesses themselves, or struggles with guilt or regret, Spirit often shows me a quarter and then flips it from heads to tails. That's their way of asking clients to look at the other side of the coin—that is, what would have happened if your shoulda/coulda/woulda/if only came true.

The great flaw in hoping you could rewrite history is that our universe is full of checks and balances; your "what if" stories always come with consequences, including the fact that no matter what, a person's destiny would cause them to pass shortly from another cause.

I'll never forget when I read a young boy who lost his father. His soul mentioned basketball and that he carries a burden around this sport. "My dad was picking me up from practice when he died in a car accident," he explained. The child had so much guilt around this, though he clearly wasn't to blame for the incident. Yet he found a way to make this his fault, as if his mind had to find some means to rationalize an otherwise senseless tragedy. This is when Spirit showed us the other side of Dad's coin: Had he survived the accident, he may have become severely injured or paralyzed, and that was not the father he wanted to be.

The next time you venture into a what-if headspace, consider whether an alternative ending is really any better. The hard truth is that your loved one died, and no matter how this happened or when, you'd always suffer from their absence. Many years ago, I read a woman whose husband passed from a heart condition. She was furious at him for ignoring how bad he felt and not seeing a doctor. She felt guilt for not forcing him to go or making the appointment herself, because she felt that had she been more of a nag, he'd be OK. Yet Spirit said, "What if you made the appointment and the doctor said I needed a triple bypass? And I stubbornly refused, as I would, and then you talked me into surgery and I never made it out of the operating room because it was my time to die? Or went home and died from a postsurgical infection? Where would the burden or guilt lie then?" Spirit said the wife would've felt she'd pushed her spouse off his cliff, so his soul chose to exit in a way that removed this emotional burden from her plate.

What's done is done.

Healing Moments

We all have a shoulda/woulda/coulda/if only that creeps into our thoughts. Write about yours in your journal, and then spend a minute thinking about the other side of the coin. Ask your loved one what might have happened had the story played out differently (and not better, this time). My guides say there's a very good chance that the first scenario that comes to mind is Spirit showing you their soul's alternative option.

18

The Blues

Feeling depressed is a natural, appropriate, and normal response to loss. I'd be worried if you *weren't* down in the dumps! When you dip in and out of funks, Spirit says to feel your way through the sadness, and ride them out until they subside each time. If you experience day in/day out depression, however, Spirit does want you to do your best to harness this, because it steals your motivation not only to do things that make you happy, but to notice that happiness exists at all. Should you worry that your depression has taken a more permanent turn, talk to an expert who can give you appropriate tools to move through your hopelessness. I'm not a therapist, but I know being depressed forever was never meant to be your fate.

No matter how temporary or gripping your depression is, have faith in your soul's ability to come back from it. Even if you start the day wondering when your heavy heart will lighten, it really helps to believe that your slump will turn around—and that a higher power will help you get there. I don't know if it's possible to manifest a mood change this way, but my guides say it puts your mind, soul, and energy in the best place for Spirit to intercede and show you opportunities that'll help you feel better. Like anger, disbelief, and all the other emotions you've met recently, melancholy will ebb and flow when you see it coming and when you don't. Know too that each time you greet depressive feelings, you will handle them better, learn from them more completely, and move through them more confidently than before.

To me, depression feels like your heart's final go at a wrenching good-bye. I think, on some level, that you know that once you work through the darkest parts of your grief, self-love and acceptance are around the corner—and you may not feel ready for that. But Spirit wants you to try.

Play Nicely

It's just as normal for you to experience depression after loss as it is for friends to want you to move through your depression. They aren't being insensitive. They love and care for you; of course they want you to feel as good as you can. The problem, to your mind, is that they'll never say what you need to hear, because they don't know what it's like to be you. They don't walk in your shoes, feel your feelings, or share your troubles. That's fine. They aren't you. But it doesn't make them worthy of outright dismissal.

Spirit says that no matter how glum you feel, you must still be kind and should give others a shot at helping you. Just because you're grieving doesn't mean you're exempt from being a good person. If someone reaches out, or asks you to tell them what you need, make the most of this! It will be good for you and them. Ask for help with errands, meals, mowing the lawn, sorting through bills. Or hey, if you need space, ask for that instead. At the very least, you can put their aid on hold but know it's there if you need it. You could say something like, "Please don't try to console me right now, because I'm in a really bad place. Just be there for me until further notice." Don't forget that you may not be alone in your depression, and a friend's offer to talk might actually be a veiled cry for help. And if you don't think their hurt is as deep as yours, think again. Everyone expresses emotions in their own way, and it's not for you to judge their suffering against yours. You are not the only person entitled to feel bad. You just aren't.

Now, if the sneaker's on the other foot and you're in the role of trying to console a grieving friend or family member, I find that the gentlest means to do this is to ask if the grieving person would like to do an activity in memory of their loved one. This can happen either in that moment or at a specific, later date so the person has an event to look forward to. Invite them to do some research on starting a foundation or scholarship in their loved one's name, gather fabric to make a memory quilt, or go flower shopping together. Don't put too much pressure on executing the entire plan—simply researching how to go about naming a park in a person's honor or what flowers grow nicely in window boxes may be enough to show that you support their process. To participate in such a project, if just in a small way, will help the person come to trust you as a confidant and feel grateful that you cared about making their day a little brighter.

All that being said, working through depression might also include distancing yourself from those who ruffle your feathers when you're having a tough day. This break doesn't have to last forever, just while you're feeling more fragile or sensitive than usual. It doesn't matter if a person's intentions are decent. If their comments are upsetting or make you feel uncomfortable, they're not good for your healing—and therefore, not good for you right now. These might include flat platitudes like "I know how you feel" (they don't) and "You'll get through this" that make you feel rotten. I'll never forget channeling a client's son who said, "Mom feels worse today than when I first died." And you know why? "When people tell me it will get better," the woman told me, "it makes me feel terrible because nothing is getting better. It reinforces my fear that I'll never heal." If you can relate, put boundaries around these encounters by spending less time with instigators or changing the subject when they're about to give advice. Help yourself emerge from this; show your strength in words and actions. As Joan

Rivers said when talking about her own grief, "I wish I could tell you it gets better, but it doesn't. *You* get better."

Depression Has a Purpose

Experts say that depression will leave once it has served its purpose. So, you ask, what's to be gained from feeling bluer than a Smurf?

For one, depression is a poignant reminder of how much you miss your loved one. I know you don't need a constant stomachache to prove you were close, but like the body's pain response, it's validation that you're hurting—and hurting because you care isn't a bad thing. Even so, Spirit often says to clients, "I know you're sad and how much you miss and love me, but I'm right here. I don't want you to focus on what I'm missing out on but everything we had together." In other words, shift your concentration from sad thoughts to happy memories and replay feel-good conversations in your mind. Researchers actually talk a lot about how the brain is capable of building and strengthening new neural connections, like when you practice piano to become a better pianist. But it also breaks down the old connections when you sleep so that your brain can empty and leave room for new connections to grow (it's called "synaptic pruning"). The amazing thing is, *you* can influence what's cleaned out during naps and at night, depending on what you focus on during the day. It's the connections you don't use that get tossed; the ones you do use actually grow and become oxygenated. So if you devote more time to going over positive memories or conversations, and less to how depressed a person's absence makes you feel, your brain will help you focus on the positive. You can fill up your brain with more good than bad.

Depression also serves the purpose of showing you how strong you can be. This might sound weird, because you probably don't feel very strong when it takes everything you've got to butter a slice of toast. But in the midst of grief, you are surviving each day—and if you are surviving, you are, in fact, showing strength and a desire (or at least willingness) to heal. In the future, your fight will not have been wasted either; you'll use this experience to inform how you deal with other kinds of sadness and struggle.

Spiritually speaking, rising above isn't a choice. Spirit expects you to return to a state of resilience after you grieve; you are meant to bounce back with faith that you can weather any storm. And who knows? Your new backbone could give you the support you need to speak out against domestic violence after your sister was murdered, or the guts to take night classes to learn how to run a business.

Spirit points out that depression can initiate bonds in unexpected ways, too. During a live show in Schenectady, New York, I read a woman named Cathie whose mother died at the age of forty-eight from pulmonary edema. At work one afternoon, she had trouble breathing and passed before she got to the hospital. "I was very sad, angry, and depressed," Cathie said. "I felt a very deep sadness knowing I couldn't talk to her one more time, that she wasn't around to answer questions when I was raising kids, and that I couldn't go shopping with her as an adult. Sometimes I'd become withdrawn, then emerge with a happy face because I had to put one on for my family. They didn't know how to deal with my sadness either."

Cathie found that leaning on her little sister Carrie—a somewhat surprising choice, given her age—was her saving grace. "I'd call Carrie, who was nineteen at the time, and we'd cry together even if we didn't know what to say. We would just stay on the line in silence until one of us thought of something to talk about." A shared understanding plus a new kind of connection helped lift Cathie's melancholy. "It also brought us closer," she said, "and we're still close to this day." And though twenty-one years have passed, Cathie still gets depressed sometimes. "When I talk about Mom, my emotions feel raw and the tears flow. Certain things come up, and I'm a mess. But on the whole, time and my talks with Carrie have eased the pain. I accept that Mom is in a better place and thank God for the years we had."

When you encounter depression, don't wait for a magical moment of closure before you feel you can move on. Spirit actually says closure isn't possible when we grieve—it's such a final term. Will you sleep better knowing your boyfriend's killer was brought to justice? Of course. Will you feel relief knowing you couldn't have stopped your father-in-law's bird flu? Most likely. Closing loops like these can help if you have open-ended questions. Otherwise closure implies that there's a neat ending to your pain, and this isn't realistic. Spirit says you can't close the door on a loved one's passing, because you can't close the door on love. So I don't think you'll ever reach a place where it no longer matters that your loved ones died, because you are never finished honoring, remembering, and loving them.

Healing Moments

Go into a meditative state, making sure to ground and protect yourself first. Think about three negative memories or conversations and three positive ones to replace them. Write them in the space provided below so that you don't have to work too hard to recall them. Before bed every night this week, relive the positive memories and engage all your senses to do so. Remember how Mom's beef bourguignon smelled, what her laugh sounded like, what her velvet sofa felt like against your legs. As time goes on, add to your catalog of positive thoughts and let sleep flush away as much *blah* as it can.

19

Pardon Me, Pardon You

You don't have to talk to dead people to instinctively know that forgiveness helps heal a shattered soul. Now you might be thinking, *That's all fine and good, but I don't have anyone to forgive.* Listen, if you've experienced any negativity related to a loved one's passing, you have someone to forgive. Spirit says forgiveness always begins with feeling mad, hurt, betrayed, resentful, burdened—sound familiar? The person doesn't need to have wronged you in a major way either. You may be annoyed at a friend for cutting out early at the wake when you needed her or frustrated at your pastor for mispronouncing your spouse's middle name during the service. You might even be disappointed with yourself for not being at the hospital when your loved one passed or second-guessing the outfit in which you laid a person to rest.

The bottom line is, where negative feelings are involved, slate cleaning is in order. It frees you of the anger that you currently feel and that perpetuates future blame, unnecessary pressure, and regret.

Spirit's a big fan of forgiveness because it supports your mind, soul, and body all at once. When you let resentments build up, your dark emotions distance you from being the best version of you. They drive a wedge between you and the purist spirit you were born with and will return to when you cross over; this is the soul God gave you to love and serve other people, plus love and be good to yourself. An inability to forgive also weighs on your health, because when you can't move past resentments, research finds that you unleash all the chemicals of a stress response—every nasty reaction releases cortisol, adrenaline, and norepinephrine in the brain. And when you think about a grudge or grievance multiple times a day? *Oof.* Those chemicals limit your ability to problem solve, causing you to feel helpless and consider yourself a victim. It's forgiveness that wipes those chemical reactions from your *whole being.* No wonder you heal!

Perhaps best of all, letting go of grievances makes room for you to experience more encouraging and uplifting feelings like happiness, hope, and discovery. Even when granting forgiveness sounds counterintuitive and kind of weird ("You upset me, but I forgive you anyway"), Spirit says it will help you heal from any situation and prevent further damage to your spiritual, emotional, and physical health.

The Three Amigos of Forgiveness

Spirit talks about three types of forgiveness—excusing others, yourself, or an upsetting situation. You may not face all three when you grieve, but there's a good chance you need to tango with at least one.

Forgiving others can be the most difficult, and Spirit calls us to do this even when we haven't received an apology from the offender first. Now, before you kick and scream about how unfair that is, this forgiving act is for *you.* It isn't something you do for the other person. When you forgive another person first, you essentially free yourself from the negative grip it can have on you. Otherwise, you huff, stew, cry, complain, wallow, possibly play the martyr, and allow it to totally subsume who you are and how you feel about yourself. You wait for an apology whose time may never come. It is a rare day that another person fully understands the magnitude of what was said and done to you, plus says all the words you need to give you the peace and ability to let go. So give yourself what others can't. And look, while you might find that forgiveness makes it palatable to spend time with the person again, you don't have to. You can still keep your distance, because forgiveness doesn't guarantee all your problems with this person are over. This is about self-protection and moving away from a situation that tortures you.

Forgiving yourself can also be an obstacle when a loved one passes, because it's so easy to question your choices after the fact. *Should I have kept Uncle Bob on life support? If I'd turned left instead of right, would I have avoided the car that ran the red light that killed my aunt?* I'll talk about *releasing* burdens and regrets in the next chapter, but for now, I need you to know that actually *forgiving* the grudge you're holding against yourself is imperative to recovering from grief. When you regret situations related to a death, you must remember: Our destiny is set. Your loved one wouldn't have pulled out of his coma if you'd given him another month to hold out for a miracle. You couldn't have controlled the oncoming car that hit you if you'd tried; in fact, you might have just slammed into a tree instead or been equally upset when your passenger died of a sudden stroke a year later. There's no productive reason to punish yourself for a death you couldn't have stopped from happening—but there *is* a productive reason to adjust your perspective and let go of the blame you've unfairly put upon yourself.

Finally, Spirit says that when our loved ones pass in tragic or freak accidents—kidnappings, murders, that kind of thing—it may be too much, at least for a while, to forgive the person who caused the death. I get that completely. And while you might hold yourself accountable in some way (*Why didn't I meet her for lunch that day instead?*), the best thing you can do is to forgive the situation. You can hate that the scenario happened, but by forgiving it, you put distance between yourself and the cause of pain. This doesn't subtract from the fact that what happened was horrible, but it can lessen the agony you feel.

"How Do You Expect Me to Forgive?"

When you forgive yourself, another person, or a situation, you aren't condoning what happened; you're accepting its reality and finding a way to live with it. Again, forgiveness is something you do for you. It has nothing to do with the person who upset you, and it isn't about forgetting what happened. It's about putting aside negative thoughts of superiority, revenge, victimhood, and fear. It is about recognizing that the adrenaline rush you feel when you're piping-mad only creates the illusion of vindication and control.

In all three forgiveness scenarios, Spirit says that you have options about how to execute them. Find a quiet time to consider the situation that upsets you and how you've been reacting to it. Forgiveness requires acknowledging what really happened, how you were affected, and what you may have contributed to the way you feel. Spirit is all about growth, so they want you to also think about whether the situation has taught you anything about yourself or what you need to be happy. Did it lend itself to meaning or opportunity in any way? Consider too why the conflict went down the way it did—is there another side to the story? Finally, think about whether you want to privately practice forgiveness or share your feelings with others. If this is better kept quiet, or if you're forgiving a loved one who's now in Heaven, you can write a letter or email and never send it or just say aloud or to yourself, "I forgive you [or myself] for [the situation]." If you prefer to have the conversation in person, the best you can do is be honest about your feelings and clear on what you hope to accomplish from the discussion. Don't go into it hoping to hear an apology or to hug it out. Approach the talk with zero expectations other than that you will feel better having gotten your emotions off your chest, and no matter what, you'll resolve to move on.

Forgiveness is meant to put a period on what happened to you so you won't feel defined or bound by it anymore. Spirit says it will bring you closer to healing, happiness, strength, and honoring yourself.

When the Person Who Wronged You Has Departed

Forgiving a loved one who's passed will release heavy feelings that keep you from moving forward. I know this is essential because, during a reading, Spirit will help the process along by sharing how much they've learned about what's causing you grief. Earlier in the book, I mentioned that when we die, our souls experience a life review process in Heaven, during which we relive the meaningful experiences that molded our journey here. We witness the behaviors, and then experience the feelings, that our choices created. Once we accept and learn from the process, our soul is able to grow because it has learned certain lessons. And I know this truly happens because a life review is what usually prompts loved ones, during readings, to apologize and take responsibility for the things they've done to hurt us. The hope, then, is that hearing a soul account for its affront leads you to forgive them. And when the soul asks for forgiveness, and then you grant it, both of your souls are rewarded with growth.

It's amazing to me that when clients are led to forgiveness, everyone needs something different. When considering forgiveness, remember that you aren't responsible for other people's choices. You can't carry burdens for what others do to you, and so forgiving a dead person is similar to forgiving someone first who's alive and doesn't plan on apologizing to you. (In fact, the deceased is likely a better audience because they always appreciate forgiving gestures and welcome your honesty!) Just say aloud or in your heart "I forgive you," and resolve to move on. You can also visualize, with your eyes closed, the person in front of you as you have the conversation you crave. Express the feelings you wish you'd said before they passed and imagine what they'd have said in response. Be sure to end your visualization on a positive note—either with a smile, a hug, or a peaceful acceptance to agree to disagree.

During a reading, I'm always impressed that Spirit knows just what will fill our emotional holes. Some need to hear that a loved one appreciated them in specific ways or is proud of the adults they've become. For others, it's that the soul owns its behaviors on earth and feels remorse. More often than not, however, it's enough for us to know that the soul understands what they did wrong and how hurt we felt, or still feel, as a result. To me, this is a much bigger lesson for every aspect of our lives—that what we need to stop hurting may not require launching foundations or lobbying Congress for change. What we crave is to feel seen, heard, and known. The path that most directly leads to this is the one to pursue.

I'll never forget when a father's soul showed me that while he was alive, he'd had a tough childhood and was a drug addict; so during his life review, he was made to relive the years of neglect, pain, and abandonment he caused—particularly to his son. Spirit showed me brief, movielike clips about this, including a scene where he said, "I'll pick you up at ten a.m. for the zoo!"—and the consequent devastation his son felt when he didn't show. During the reading, Dad's soul said to his son, "I'm sorry I couldn't be the father you needed, and deserved, for me to be. I didn't know how to unconditionally love, but I am learning that in Heaven." Hearing those words, I could energetically feel the son forgive his dad; he was grateful that at least as a soul, Dad has the wisdom to see his faults and has a willingness to improve. His dad went on to admit that he didn't realize how much damage he caused until he saw and experienced it for himself. Spirit says we should own our choices, but if we don't or can't within reason, we have the chance to take accountability in Heaven. Note that had the man chosen not to forgive his father's plea, he still could have forgiven the situation or even himself for holding a grudge—your soul welcomes whatever is most comfortable for you. Even with forgiveness, God gives you choices that mesh with how you feel.

I should add too that forgiveness has implications not just for your life now but for your future karma. To continue with this father/son example, because the departed soul grew from its mistakes, and the son forgave him, which helps his own soul grow, this relationship dysfunction/lesson isn't one that each soul will have to repeat in a future life or work out when they're both in Heaven together. The lesson is complete, and so there's no unfinished business between them. The two can move on to other lessons in a more enlightened state, plus a more fulfilling and positive relationship in their next life together.

Spirit says that what might help you forgive a person who's passed is to know that while your soul retains the core of your personality, it is given copious opportunities to return to its best state—in other words, you may have acted like a jerk on earth, but once you're in Heaven, it's hard to stay a jerk for long. You are pure, once again. Perhaps it's because I channel souls that walk in God's light, but none are so damaged that they're beyond remorse or refuse chances to redeem themselves through life reviews, guiding loved ones, karmic opportunities, and so on. A touching example of this, which comes up a lot actually, is when wives care for their dying husbands in a nursing capacity—and the ailing spouse rarely says thanks. Spirit will show me how the wife puts on a brave face but then secretly cries or breaks down over how she felt she'd been treated. Yet in Heaven, departed souls feel at once grateful for how difficult their spouses' job was and how insensitively they may have behaved. They'll say, "Theresa, she did so much for me, and never once did I thank her or tell her how much I appreciated it. For that, I am sorry." This helps the person on earth relinquish any negative feelings they may have harbored around this—from anger at the departed to guilt over that anger. At this point, both Spirit's and the wife's souls are set free.

Healing Moments

In your journal, list three people or situations connected to your loved one's departure that you know, in your soul, will help you heal or grow from your grief if you forgive them. Be truthful about what occurred and if you had any part to play in either how the situation transpired or how you responded to it. In the next week, practice forgiveness in your mind, in a prayer to God, during meditation, or to the person directly. How did it go? How did it make you feel? Write about the experience with honesty and perspective.

20

Take Care

I know getting a good amount of rest, eating your veggies, making time for exercise, drinking plenty of water, taking your vitamins, and getting fresh air sounds like a tall order right now. And I am well aware that your main objective may be to just get through the day without a nervous breakdown in Macy's underwear department. But when you're grieving, it's so, so, so important to take care of yourself as best you can. Although the grief process typically involves a lot of sleeping and unintentional calorie reduction, the energy behind it is depleting to your system. Feeling so physically, emotionally, and mentally taxed exhausts your whole being and makes it hard for your soul to heal. It also makes it tough to fight off viruses and bacteria, bad moods, and other people's negativity when you come across it. All I'm saying is that you need more problems like you need a hole in the head. So if you hope to embrace life and heal your soul, you need to put forth a certain amount of positive effort and intention devoted to *you*.

Enough Really *Is* Enough

When you feel your absolute best, your mind, body, and soul are in perfect balance—but perfection is not what you're going for right now. Your goal while grieving is to feel balanced enough. This means doing as much as you can to feel good, since neglecting just one of these three areas throws the others off kilter. But becoming an ace at all three? That's too unrealistic and time-consuming for life as you know it.

Here's what imbalance can look like, so you'll know why you want to avoid it. So first, maybe a few physical symptoms crop up—fatigue, depression, weight gain or loss, aches and pains, rashes, insomnia, and other signs of lowered immunity. Then maybe your thinking or emotional processing becomes scrambled or foggy, and before you know it, you lose faith in your ability to heal and begin to doubt your inner voice. As time goes on, it gets harder to get back to your baseline, so you throw up your hands altogether. Please, don't go there if you can help it. Right now you need to feel strong, capable, and able to rely on the innate mechanisms God gives you to feel better. But you have to do your part too.

After a loss, the perfect storm of sorrow, fatigue, and apathy can keep you from good health habits. Trust me, you are not the first person to think, *What's the worst that can happen if I live on Entenmann's crumb cakes?* "After my husband, Brian, died, I didn't give a rip about anything," a fan named Jenn shared. "Everyone took me out to dinner, and I constantly drank wine because I couldn't cope. I was too exhausted to exercise, plus Brian wasn't there to join me at the gym or take a walk. I was on antidepressants that fed weight gain too. Three years later, I was up thirty pounds and felt horrible." On top of it, Jenn was too taxed to logically maneuver through the well-intentioned enabling of others, like when her friend who'd also lost his partner took her out for lunch. "I'll never forget it," she said. "I ordered a salad, and he stopped me and said, 'Give yourself some love. Order something comforting.' I ordered this big meat dish with mashed potatoes instead—a lunch I'd have never eaten normally. His words became my mantra: 'Haven't I been through enough? I have to diet now too?' And I really paid for it." I'm not saying don't order a slice of pie once in a while, but there are better ways to nourish yourself from the inside out.

Listen, this is not the time to go on a cleanse or overhaul your diet either. I want you to make small adjustments. Go slow. Your goal isn't to be a cover model; it's to be healthy enough. In practice, this means that if you don't have it in you to steam vegetables for dinner—because seriously, who does—drink a green juice a few days a week. If you can't make it to the gym, go for a walk or at least stretch outside in the clear, fresh air. When people ask if they can make you meals, request nourishing pots of soup, roasted vegetables, and crusty breads. You don't have to wear makeup, but use natural moisturizers that replenish your skin. Keep a bottle of lemon water nearby for when you're thirsty. Wind down with a cup of tea before an early bedtime. Positive baby steps like these will support you just enough to maintain your health and raise your energy so your body, mind, and soul are given their best shot to heal. And when you *are* ready to go back to the gym or cook for yourself again, you'll have a head start.

Let Others Care for You

Don't be afraid to ask for help when you can't do for yourself. TLC should come from people you know and those you don't. Grief can cause us to push family and friends away, or keep them at a distance, and if that's what you need for a bit, fine—it won't be forever. But don't isolate yourself from *all* human interaction entirely. Also unhealthy: limiting your relationships to counselors or fellow mourners who only want to talk about grief. Once in a while, it's nice to take some time off from what brings you down.

Spirit says to look for practitioners who will take care of you and whom you'll enjoy seeing on a regular basis. Consider standing appointments with a massage or bodywork therapist who can offer a calming touch or an acupuncturist who can help balance your energy and overall health. Even a ten-dollar foot rub at the nail salon can ease your burdens. To be honest, sometimes seeing a practitioner is more comforting than a friend or family member because you don't feel obligated to interact the same way—and yet you might open up and feel more loved than you thought possible.

I also like the idea of a caring personal trainer if you can afford it—even once a week is helpful—or make it a point to walk for at least half an hour a few days a week (outside, at the gym, with a friend, alone . . .). I can't tell you how important I think it is to make sure you get some kind of physical exercise while you're grieving. It's good for your body's health, but it also cleanses the energy in and around you. Instead of giving off gray, ugly, negative energy, you give off higher, brighter light. It helps your mental outlook too. When we exercise, our brains naturally produce neurotransmitters like serotonin, dopamine, glutamate, and GABA—not to mention endorphins, which are chemicals that play a key role in blocking pain and controlling emotions and mood. They're responsible for certain feelings related to happiness. It's like the line in *Legally Blonde* when the lead character Elle says, while defending a fitness instructor accused of murder, "Exercise gives you endorphins. Endorphins make you happy. Happy people just don't shoot their husbands!" In the same way, Spirit says happy people just don't grieve the same as unhappy people, and endorphins help! Look, I'm a generally positive person, but when I'm in the worst mood, I find that exercise is a godsend. Mid-workout, I feel better, and by the end, I feel good for *at least* the rest of the day. I also have a clearer head to process any other crappy feelings that come my way.

You know how Spirit and I suggested that you check in with yourself when you want to self-soothe? You can do the same when it comes to figuring out how to support yourself. Ask, *What do I need to do, or whom do I need to see, to take care of myself today?* Listen to what your body and soul tell you.

Healing Moments

In your journal, jot down five things you can do to help boost your health. Ideas: add a "superfood" like spinach or blueberries to your lunch, get at least eight hours of sleep a night, make an appointment to see a craniosacral therapist who works with grief. . . . Then, for a week, try each one out and enjoy how it feels to take care of yourself. Consider making the ones you liked best a habit. You'll notice a real difference!

21

Tell Your Truth

Whether I'm happy, sad, confused, or pissed off, it doesn't matter. I need to express myself. This makes me feel lighter, plus nobody ever has to wonder how I'm feeling because I volunteer this info first! And if I don't blurt out my emotions, I find that I inevitably show them by what I'm wearing, how my hair looks, or what songs I listen to on the radio. But I know that not everyone is like me, especially when grieving. Some people go quiet and keep to themselves, and that's OK too.

Yet while silence and contemplation have their place, Spirit says that finding productive ways to convey how you feel can help dissolve your heartache. Self-expression can include talking till you're blue in the face, or using a more creative format that gives your soul a voice: painting, singing, writing, photography, cooking, and so on. What matters is that in the process, you explore and communicate how you feel and what makes you tick. And don't think for a second that self-expression is just a onetime conversation or craft project. Your story, feelings, and experiences change as you do. You're a work in progress, and so is your journey through grief and the way you choose to illustrate it over and over again.

When you express yourself, you control the narrative and keep the door open to your loved one's life. Pouring out your heart feels cathartic, memorializes your loved one, and takes the onus off others to guess how you're feeling. When you're hurt, nobody can seem to say the right thing, at the right time, or in the right way. They do not know how you are feeling minute to minute, just as *you* don't know how you'll feel minute to minute. But when you tell your truth, you not only explain what's going on inside but also clue others in to how you need to be supported. Sharing a heartfelt side of you also tells them that it's OK to mention the deceased and invites them to share their memories too.

It's Not Just About the Pain

No matter how you choose to express yourself, try not to make pain the constant or sole focus of cathartic expression. How many times do you have to replay a hurtful scene in your mind, or a mistake you regret being part of, before you make yourself sick? Spirit says to give equal time to comforting memories and uplifting details for an evenhanded but realistic portrayal of your emotional landscape. So when you're considering whether to paint a picture about how your now-deceased grandfather screamed at you while suffering from a painful UTI in the hospital, or how, in his final moments, you sat by his bed at home, held his hand, and exchanged "I love you"s before he closed his eyes to pass—well, you can guess which story Spirit prefers you portray, not just because it feels comforting to you but will to others too.

I know that asking you not to focus on pain, *when you're in pain*, can sound like an insensitive or far-fetched request. But you have to realize that grief is not the enemy here. It is your response to a painful situation, and if you support your grief, perhaps it will better support you. It's like how, when you're sick, spirituality experts suggest you "send love to your body"—even when you feel like your body's letting you down. The thinking here is that if you prop yourself up with every ounce of compassion you have, your body, mind, and soul will absorb your positive intentions and use them to support you. So in that vein, Spirit says it may help to send love to your grief. You can do this by visualizing yourself in a bubble of pink light, which is the color I associate with love; slowly breathe it in and imagine it circulating throughout your body on the exhale, particularly around your heart. You could also write grief a letter, telling it how you feel, from a position of positivity and strength. Something like:

Dear Grief,

I know you'll always be here, and right now I don't like the way you make me feel. But I know that you will also make me stronger, and I will soon heal with your help. I know you're just doing your job, but I would rather you support me than take me down when I miss Grandma.

Love you,
Theresa

What would you lovingly say to your grief if you had the chance?

Use Your Words

I truly believe that God puts assistance in our path when we ask for it, and usually in unexpected ways. Remember too that different types of support work at different stages of grief. In the beginning, you might crave the company, empathy, and stories of others but eventually wish to grieve more privately. Try to be mindful of what you need in that moment—maybe a friend who gives pep talks versus one who lets you just talk and cry. Every person in your circle should have something special to share.

Though talking about your grief is the most common way to express your feelings, it becomes harder when you worry about upsetting those around you or making people uncomfortable. If this crosses your mind, Spirit says not to worry about how others react and to tell them what to expect from you, should you find yourself in a situation that becomes awkward. I used to do this when I'd go out with my friends and I was suffering from crippling anxiety; I never knew how I'd react when I was away from home, which was my safety zone, so I'd warn everyone ahead of time about what might go down (panic attacks, a sudden need to flee—oh, it was a real adventure to have dinner with me back then!). So in your case, if you accept a lunch invite but worry you'll cry in your chicken salad, or that your friend will make a comment that pisses you off (or that she won't say anything at all) . . . just tell it like it is, and how it could be, so that nothing is delicate or alarming in the moment. If you break down, you break down, and if not, everyone's good with it. Spirit suggests saying something like, "I'm having a bad day, and I'm not sure how I'll feel at lunch, so if I cry or start talking about Uncle Jim, bear with me. I'll be OK. If you want to ask me a question, go ahead. Don't feel like you have to walk on eggshells."

Healthy communication includes telling others when you need to be left alone too. Your loved ones only want to help, but they rarely know what to say and do on their own. They need to be told when to engage and when to back off. Be kind about this, and they'll appreciate the guidance. A simple "I don't know what I need right now, so please just be there for me" can put the other person on notice. The best you can do is speak from the heart and hope your allies are with you. What you don't want is to put a guard up, so that your health and relationships, which *could* have been supportive, now suffer.

Get Creative

I also like the idea of creative expression at any point in your grief process. Writing, painting, drawing, playing or singing music, dancing, cooking, taking photos . . . these are all satisfying ways to pour your guts into something productive. The end result doesn't have to look professional, realistic, or go for a lot of money at an auction. Creative grieving is for *you*. It's the process and emotional release that matter. Healing comes from the doing, not from the result—though who knows? You might surprise yourself. My friend Marie-Christine told me a great story about how she got into baking when her aunt Nelly died. "My Peruvian aunt had a cookie business making *alfajores*, and they were amazing," she said. "To help me grieve, I did research and found an *alfajores* recipe, put on some fun Peruvian music, and made the cookies from scratch—something I'd never done before. I got to think about her and the fun times we had, and I got some awesome cookies out of it. Not as good as Aunt Nelly's, but still good!"

A lot of clients talk about writing a book related to their journeys, so I wouldn't be surprised if you've thought of it too! If this is the case, I encourage you to stay open to different genres beyond memoir as you consider what you've been through and how far you've come—be it self-help, spiritual, even a fictionalized account of your experiences. I absolutely adore what Abby Fabiaschi did when she wrote the novel *I Liked My Life*. "Eight years before it was published," Abby said, "the book began as a way to process losing one of my best friends, Elizabeth, who died in a car accident when we were in high school." Parlaying the experience into fiction helped Abby feel a little more in control, during a time when she felt she had very little. "It was wholly cathartic. And as I wrote, I felt Elizabeth there with me," she said. "At first it freaked me out—was I exploiting my grief and her life with the project?—but the chills I got at certain points were so clearly supportive, like she was cheering me on."

Though the book initially set out to explore the anger, confusion, and guilt of a hormonal teen grappling with grief, Abby's work took a turn when her own life did. During revisions, her dad died from a heart attack—it was sudden and unexpected. "He was my father, but also my boss, mentor, and best friend, so his exit left a big hole," she said. Abby was so beside herself, she put her book aside for three years. "Then one day I happened upon it on my computer, and it felt enormously important to revisit. I was desperate to keep my dad's voice alive, so I poured it into a strong, male character." Writing, and rewriting, her book was a journey of love, loss, and healing. "I sob during sad movies or with friends having a hard time, but I never cry when the loss is mine," Abby said. "Writing has become a way for me to unburden my loss on unsuspecting characters." Though Abby chose to express herself on paper, your medium is up to you. What matters to Spirit is that you expel your grief in a way that cleanses your soul.

Healing Moments

Get your grief out in a way you never have before. So if you talk about your feelings a lot, sketch an abstract picture with colored pencils that portrays how you feel, or photograph all the flower arrangements you've been sent in various stages of their life cycle. Maybe you want to use Play-Doh to sculpt the signs Spirit sends you, like the two blue jays that sit on your windowsill every morning. You could even write a goofy song or a spooky poem about how your pet senses Spirit's energy. Get into it, and enjoy!

22

Go Au Natural

When was the last time you hiked near a waterfall, spread out with a delicious picnic, or strolled along a pristine beach during sunset and thought, *YUCK! This place is disgusting. The sound of water stresses me out! The freshly cut grass smells awful! The colors in the sky are the most vile I've ever seen!*

What? That's never happened? Yeah, that's my point. Whether you prefer to be surrounded by colorful flowers or majestic mountains, nature is known to have transformative effects on your entire being. You don't have to be outside for long before you feel invigorated by the fresh air, all five senses have started to hum, and you feel connected to the earth. Your overall energy perks up. Remember, everything in the universe is made from energy and vibrates at different frequencies. Spirit says being around positive types of energy, like that in nature, can lighten the heavier feelings that come with struggles.

So venture outside and enjoy God's creation. Don't forget the bug spray!

Healing Vibes

When choosing outdoor activities, keep this in mind: The more you immerse yourself in Mother Nature, the more you stand to benefit. For example, swimming in a huge ocean, holding powerful stones, or full-on hugging a tree will touch your soul more deeply than running outside to get the mail or seeing the sun only when you pick up your child from preschool. In fact, there's a practice called grounding that has beautiful healing effects; you might want to try it! All you have to do is walk outside in bare feet (or cotton socks) for about half an hour to reconnect with the earth's subtle, natural, electrical energy and allow it to flow directly into your body. You can do this on the grass, sand, dirt, or concrete. Your immune system and its healing mechanisms—including those related to your emotions—function best when your body has enough electrons, which are said to be easily and naturally obtained this way. These electrons have an anti-inflammatory effect, and their energy helps keep your body's innate electrical circuitry balanced. Research also shows that grounding can improve heart rate, cortisol dynamics, sleep, your nervous system, and stress! None of this should be too surprising, since Spirit says the earth is chock full of stones and minerals that affect our energy. Think of how your hands tingle when you hold a chunk of elestial quartz or how relaxed you feel after taking a magnesium supplement. The earth's vibrations have a powerful presence in God's natural elements.

A lot of my clients also like to experience the earth through gardening. I credit Mother Earth's healing properties with how good this can make you feel. It's like that kids' saying, "God made dirt, so dirt don't hurt!"—in fact, it's really great for you! Digging into rich soil connects you with the planet, and there's something to be said for embracing the symbolic life cycle of vegetables, flowers, and plants; they remind us that beauty, death, and rebirth are part of every life form here. It's also therapeutic to have a ritualistic way to lose yourself in prettiness and productivity. And while a lot of my clients love to design and take care of gardens as a way to honor their loved ones, I'll never forget the woman I read who buried her husband's cremains in the garden behind her house. She was about to move, and the man's soul showed me a little vaselike urn, with dirt being brushed off it, as a reminder to bring him along! Can you *imagine* leaving cremains behind? Or, OMG, finding them as the new owner? I'm so glad Spirit spoke up!

When Nature Calls

I don't think it's a coincidence that some of Spirit's most beloved signs come from nature. Butterflies, feathers, birds, ladybugs, flowers, wild animals—they're accessible ways for your loved ones to tell you they're around because they're quick to recognize, readily available for Spirit to use, and give us instant happiness! It's like when my client saw a double rainbow over his house the day of his father's funeral, and it hadn't even rained! And then there's my friend Anna who associates a specific bird call with her mother, because one of her favorite memories from childhood is when she'd come downstairs in the mornings to hear her mom talking to a family of birds she's since learned were bright red cardinals; their call sounded to her like *pret-ty, pret-ty, pret-ty, pret-ty.* . . . Wouldn't you know, shortly after her mother died, Anna was sitting on the back porch when she heard the call—so loud, it sounded like it was chirping right in her ear. Anna instantly knew, *That's from Mom!* And now she mostly hears the bird when she's in a situation that makes her long for reassurance and comfort. Anna knows it's her mom saying everything will be OK.

I get my fair share of nature signs too. My grandmother on my dad's side, Nanny Brigandi, sends me big, fat houseflies when she wants to say hi and Gram drops bunnies in my path. I can't help but smile when I see either one. You know, maybe Spirit communicates with me like this because I've always felt connected to Native American culture (I have a warrior guide that I call "Chief"), which values its bond with nature. In fact, they believe we all have nine animal guides that walk with us through life. Can you imagine what my totem pole would look like with a giant, hairy fly face on it? That's so my life.

Healing Moments

Spend a week trying new nature-based activities and jot down what you get out of each one. In your journal, make a chart with two columns. In the first, write down the activity, and in the second, a word that describes how it made you feel. Maybe walking barefoot through dandelions makes you feel momentarily carefree. Or how the methodical cutting of spring flowers from your yard is calming but creative. That's the great thing about nature—no one activity or environment elicits the same response in everyone, and your reaction might evolve over time too. At the end of the week, you will have an emotionally strategic guide for the next time you want to get out and feel good.

23

Be There for the Living

For as often as Spirit tells you to be good to yourself, they also insist that you "don't forget about the living." This is one of the many reasons they urge you to keep up your health and spirits—so you have the bandwidth to be there for others. I'm not suggesting you spend a two-hour lunch counseling your friend about her ex-boyfriend drama or pretending to care about her new curtains, but if you have kids, friends, animals, or family members that need your attention, this is not the time to let that part of your life go.

When Helping Others Helps You

It's normal to become so caught up in your grief that you're tempted to neglect or dismiss those around you. Whether you realize it or not, you might overlook the needs of loved ones and pets that rely on you to thrive. Or you might simply become so steeped in sadness that you forget to tell your support system how much you appreciate them. Because it's hard to see beyond your own heartache, I always insist during my live shows that audience members (who are usually in the throes of grief) turn to the person they came with, thank them for coming, and tell these patient human beings how much they love them. Feeling grateful and putting yourself out for others is always a muscle worth training, and because of what you're going through right now, it will take deliberate practice. Know too that it's worth the effort.

The upside for you, Spirit says, is that being forced to show up for those around you can be a boon to your healing. Like it or not, it gives you an incentive to learn how to coexist with your sadness because you can't ignore that the cat needs to be fed or your daughter needs help with her homework; life doesn't stop because you're grieving. And so you have to push on. I once read a woman on *Long Island Medium* named Lisa whose daughter Jennica died in a car accident on Christmas Day, shortly after she turned sixteen years old. Jennica was in their Jeep Cherokee with her brother Justin, on their way to celebrate the holiday with their dad—and despite Justin's very best efforts, he lost control of the vehicle when he hit a patch of black ice. This caused the vehicle to roll over a very steep snowbank and crash into a tree. Jennica died instantly, and if it weren't for the fact that the tree stopped them from tipping over the edge, Lisa believes Justin would have died too.

Because Lisa had to care for her deeply grieving son, "I didn't have a choice when it came to being there for him," she said. "It was truly an accident, and I couldn't let him feel like he killed me too. He was only eighteen when this happened." Initially to help them both cope, Lisa said, "I tried to keep my emotions to myself as much as possible. When Justin was not at the house, there were times I found it extremely hard to function." Even so, Lisa says caring for her son, and helping him find his way, helped her discover the strength to climb out of their shared, personal hell. "Justin had enough to deal with," she told me, "and if he felt like I stopped trying, I was afraid he'd stop trying too. I often think God spared Justin so that I could continue my will to live." During this time, Lisa also reached out to families who'd lost a child, and still does, to help impart the hard-earned lessons she's learned. Extending herself like this has allowed her grief to become productive—if you can be a teacher, you don't feel like just a victim.

Justin, on the other hand, felt it was impossible to be there for others because "many of the people who needed me were a reminder of our loss." He says, "I couldn't carry on a conversation with my family, because seeing them sad was a constant reminder of the pain they felt—a pain I felt I'd played a part in. Rather than have to witness the pain, and try to help them through it, I wanted to be alone." He felt empty inside and assumed he couldn't help even if he tried. "I was numb in a lot of ways, and needing to have an emotional response to anyone when you're feeling absolutely nothing is a difficult thing to deal with," Justin said. "I think I felt this way because I was ultimately scared of losing someone else. It was easier to avoid attention or caring so I didn't have to build any more emotional attachments to someone I might lose. I was living on autopilot." Eventually, however, Justin was able to open up and talk to others about his situation—and he realized that being part of a mutually supportive dialogue helped him feel better. As he wisely put it, "Grief is not an experience that anyone should have alone."

Both Justin and his mom, Lisa, have made tremendous strides in their healing process, and I can't tell you how proud I am of them both. "Eventually I came to realize that you don't get to choose the order of life's events," Justin said. "That no amount of agonizing was going to bring Jennica back or change what happened. I knew I had to just keep moving, one day at a time." Justin says he thinks of his sister throughout the day, and it helps him carry on. "I run across little hints that she's near or things happen that make me think of her," he said, "and I always try to think of how happy she must be in a better place." Lisa is grateful for both her son's strength and the memories she has of her daughter. "We had an amazing relationship. I believe God blessed me with that, knowing she'd have such a short life on earth."

It's All About Love

You might think caring for others is healing because it's a healthy distraction or break from your own pain, but what really mends the soul here is the exchange of love that occurs between you and the person who needs you. When you grieve, the person you're helping feels appreciative and sends love back to you, and then you're fed too. Back and forth it goes, like a Ping-Pong ball. And when you put others first, you aren't just pouring your toddler a bowl of cereal or helping your ninety-eight-year-old mom up the stairs; you are strengthening your love, and it's a bond that only gets stronger for eternity. Frankly, when you're called to push through your own devastation to serve another, the *only* place this effort could come from is one of love. The grieving heart has no room for duty, obligation, and "doing the right thing."

If you're not needed in a critical way, you may find it healing to care for strangers. In no way am I suggesting that you try to outrun your pain by doing or going as fast as you can. But when you feel severed and sore, performing acts of love and kindness can be a helpful tool in your healing kit. Maybe you could help out in a way that's related to your loved one's passing, like raising money for research related to their cause of death—or assist in an unrelated way, like driving your neighbor to the doctor and having lunch after. Perhaps you'd like to channel all your pent-up emotions into a physically grueling purpose, like doing the weekly landscaping for your church or working at an orphanage in a third-world country. All these examples ask you to focus on love, rather than grief, and that is a healing swap.

At some point soon, you will be back on the receiving end of service and love. The karmic boomerang always circles back to you. Remember, then, what it is to be a gracious recipient. When you feel like nobody understands what you're going through, it's easier to feel self-conscious about your behavior than tell yourself there's no other way. Spirit says the best thing to do when these feelings crop up is to just pause and receive. Let yourself feel loved, and your heart will gradually expand and heal.

Healing Moments

Tell someone you love how much you appreciate them, and if you've been angry, also tell them that you're sorry for the way you've acted and take responsibility for it. Explain what's going on in your head—what you're feeling, what your days look like, how it compares to other traumas you've experienced, and that you know you're not being yourself but want to thank them for being there and trying to help. Nobody can truly know the depths of the suffering you've endured, and sometimes I find that we have to really paint a detailed picture for others to get it. The result is a stronger bond built on honesty and communication.

24

Don't Be Scared

Fear attacks us in so many ways when we grieve; it makes concerns we already have worse, not to mention creates and feeds new ones. It's hard enough to handle everyday stress—wondering what your blood work will show, or if your kid will get picked for his school play—but when fear underscores anguish? *Madonne.* You already feel emotionally taxed, and now you have to find the mental clarity and stability to make sense of the unknown. It's a miracle that any of us ever leaves the house on a regular basis.

I personally know a lot about fear and how it can roll into full-blown panic and inertia, because it dominated a good chunk of my life for twenty-five years. During this time, I suffered from what therapists call "anticipatory anxiety"—in other words, thinking about future events made me feel anxious and interfered with my ability to function. I never wanted to leave the house or go out with friends, and I was constantly afraid that something bad was going to happen to me. To make things worse, I didn't know what would trigger a freak-out, feed the fear-driven loop in my head, or make these feelings go away. For me, I came to learn that my overwhelming anxiety was occurring because I was ignoring Spirit energy that was trying to com-

municate with me, though I didn't realize it at the time. All I knew
was that something was affecting me in such a way that I'd become
short of breath, my heart would start racing, and I'd feel my throat
close up—and I had no idea why. So I kept fear at a minimum by
trying to dodge it, which meant either hiding out at home or running
for my life when I felt uncomfortable in public.

Though I realize your fears have a different cause, our distress and
panic actually have a lot in common. Like you, my worst fears came
from not being able to see the truth of a situation and later accept it,
permitting my negative emotions to establish an even firmer grip on
me. Fear also caused a physical reaction in me that, after a while, made
it hard for me to tell what prompted what. So for me, I couldn't figure
out if a situation or person or health issue was causing me to panic and
lose my breath, or if losing my breath caused me to panic even more;
but for you, it might be that since your mom died, you're afraid to
have kids and you can't tell whether her passing caused this reaction or
brought old doubts to light. What I eventually did learn—and I know
you will too—was that while I thought fear was happening *to* me, I
was actually choosing to react to situations in a fearful way. It wasn't
until I started looking for answers about how to truly heal myself that
I found my way out of the darkness.

What Are You Afraid Of?

The thing about fear is that you can feel it in just about any situation—and once it digs in its claws, it seems hard to shake. So when
fear encroaches on your grieving process, it becomes logistical (maybe
you can't hold down a job while you're emotionally struggling), or
reactionary (can't be around new people), and/or practical (can't drive
long distances because your partner usually took the wheel, or pay
bills, since you never handled finances before). You might even spin
imaginative, far-out fears, like your deceased mother must be dev-

astated that your son is gay or your dead husband is depressed that you remarried. There are also fears about the future—if the life you wanted is no longer in the cards, what is?—plus your own destiny.

It's fascinating that nearly all my clients face fears about love. They are both afraid of it and crave it, and I guess this is because when you lose someone, that's what goes missing. Spirit says love can then become elusive and scary to think about feeling again. Clients become nervous to love or be loved, or participate in gestures of love like holding hands or expressing emotions. I remember reading a woman who was afraid to let her boyfriend fully love her because it might lead to marriage—and the reason was that she couldn't fathom walking down the aisle without her dad around. I've also read a woman who, because her brother died unexpectedly, feared she'd suddenly lose whomever else she tried to love. In both cases, Spirit told these women to "release your fears and allow yourself to be loved the way you deserve." Their family's souls wanted them to still receive the love that they were no longer here to provide.

No matter what, remember that fears are a normal response to grief, but they only go away if you recognize and work on the ones that affect you most. No fear has to become part of who you are. Just like the fear you feel on the first day of a new job or after breaking up with a boyfriend, this too shall pass as you heal. In time, some of your fears will go away on their own, others will disappear when you address them, and still others may require help. New fears will crop up. Don't run, but handle these as they come.

"*I'm* Not Fearful!"

Fear is a lot like anger, in that the word can encompass so many more feelings than you already associate it with. Sometimes, then, it's easier to identify your fears according to what you *do* rather than what you *think you feel*. Once in a while, a client will say to me, "I don't have fear, Theresa"—and then three breaths later say, "I don't know what to do. I can't stop crying!" To me and Spirit, it's clear that this person is extremely afraid that she'll never discover her new normal, but she might not see it this way. All she knows is that she feels conflicted, confused, and weepy—but these are all signs of a larger fear.

Behavioral signs of fear aren't that hard to spot; you just have to open your eyes to them. Isolation is a typical reaction to fear when you're grieving. So is feeling anxious, helpless, and insecure. Panic attacks are also common, since they're essentially a stockpile of negative emotions that take you down at once. Another sign of fear is distrusting God and your existing beliefs—faith and fear, of course, cannot logically coexist. Just be careful, because if you allow your fears to snowball, they can become harder to recognize. What once began with the fear *Did my sister suffer?* can turn into *I'll never love anyone like her again.* If your behavior reflects fear, work backward from the reaction and ask yourself, *Why do I feel this way? What can I do, or who can I talk to, to help me get through this?* Behavioral fear is your body's response to a threatening situation, and with practice, you can choose a different one.

Face the Fears You Face

The best thing you can do when you notice fear in yourself is deal with it head-on; from there, it will gradually fade away. If you ignore it, hide it, or let it build up, your fear doesn't go anywhere; you are now just alone with your fear, which is when it takes on a life of its own. Your fears become bigger than they are and need to be. However, when you honestly and openly think about, identify, and verbalize what worries you—whether it's to a trusted friend or therapist, to a pastor or in prayer, to your loved one via a letter, or to yourself in a journal—then you no longer dwell on what's going on inside. Don't give fear the power to control your inner monologue—the things we tell ourselves on a daily basis are what motivate our thoughts and actions. Expose your fear, move through it. I don't have a pat answer to how you can accomplish this, because our fears are all so personal. But Spirit says that as you earnestly try to overcome fear, you will take back the paralyzing control that fear has over you, and that's half the battle.

A good starting point for anyone is forward motion. Choosing something—anything—to do that will shift the energy around you. This doesn't need to be a life-changing decision to meet another person by going on Match.com or find a new job that fulfills your greatest purpose. Spirit suggests a task that turns the page and gives you something to think about beyond your sadness. Regardless of your age, get a part-time job or an internship that makes you happy to get up each day—say, at a florist or candy maker. If I were in this situation, I'd work in a bakery and make bread all day—who am I kidding, I'd get a job at Christian Louboutin for the discount! Your goal is to find a pleasantly tolerable experience that makes you part of the living and gets you out of your head. This will give you a healthy sense of control and expose you to new people and a feeling of normalcy. *Oh right*, you'll think. *This is what life is. I almost forgot.* You'll meet people who are coping with their own issues—health, divorce, childhood traumas, finance issues . . . everyone's got their something: watch how they make it part of their life without it becoming the focal point. You'll find support, inspiration, invitations, and opportunities in unexpected places.

In the end, Spirit tells clients to let go of their fears, which is another way of giving you their blessing—and asking you to give *yourself* permission—to live in a different way. In execution, the act of letting go can be different for everyone based on their fears and belief system. For some, letting go means surrendering to God's plan and accepting that all fears related to a person's death are related to the lessons your soul must learn. To others, letting go means making a conscious decision to feel, think, and behave differently by saying, "You know what? I'm not going to let fear control my life." When a person dies, you lose everything—so your next step can't be to fear the unknown but to figure out how to rebuild and go on.

Healing Moments

In your journal, Spirit would like you to write a letter to your loved one that examines one pressing fear and how it stems from, or relates to, your grief process. How does this fear make you feel? Even if it's warranted, is it helping you to dwell on it or causing you harm? Are you making any progress by holding on to this fear? What's at the core of it all? When you're finished writing, tear the letter from your book—fear has no place in your healing journal!—and burn it somewhere safe, like in your driveway. Then take ten minutes to sit quietly and consider how you can emotionally and actively let go of fear. What would realistically help you move forward? What would your loved one tell you to do about how you feel?

25

It's Just Stuff—Or Is It?

Deciding what to do with your loved one's things, and when to tackle this enormous project, can feel overwhelmingly sentimental and difficult. And if you're not tasked with doling stuff out but hope to be on the receiving end in some way, it's an awkward waiting game at best and can put a strain on your relationships if the situation isn't handled tactfully. No wonder grief counselors tell you to sort through belongings shortly after a loved one dies! I say, don't rush it if you don't have to. For some, going through the motions of sifting through tangible memories will help them come to peace with a departure, but many need to find acceptance before being able to tackle this project. The truth is, your soul will tell you how to handle this—when, with whom, and how to divvy things up—when the time is right for you.

And just so you know going into this project, Spirit has *a lot* to say about their stuff, but it's always to reinforce that they support the choices you've made or are about to make. I know this sounds like a feel-good reassurance, but it's not. It's their way of saying that what we do with their belongings isn't for them but to help us find peace. Spirit has never said to me that they miss their letterman jacket or can't believe Aunt Linda got the sapphire ring! Not to sound rude, but they really don't care about physical things, just like they don't miss their bodies, because there's nothing tangible about life in Heaven; thoughts and feelings prevail there. It's a lot like how Spirit feels about laying their human forms to rest. They're grateful that we make the effort, but whether we bury them, spread their cremains, or wear their ashes in a necklace doesn't matter to Spirit. The choice is meant to bring *us* peace.

The only thing on this plane that matters to Spirit is you.

Finders, Keepers

Deciding what to give away and covet yourself can be a little tough to parse out. It's tempting to want to keep every little thing that makes you tear up and pings your heart—Meemaw's Tupperware! Aunt Julie's porcelain ballerina collection!—but you need to make choices. And don't hold on to things because you don't want others to have them; death isn't yet another opportunity to play "finders keepers, losers weepers" with your siblings. Instead, Spirit says it's a good idea to keep things you can currently use like a teapot, throw blanket, or even a purse and sunglasses that really defined your loved one's style and now can be part of yours. I still have Gram's china, for instance, and I use it on holidays and for Sunday dinner. I'd also hold on to items that remind you of the person's essence and reflects their personality—clothing, a stuffed animal, a painting, an antique mirror—so you feel close to them when you see it. Items that can wrap around you, like a sweater or blanket, can bring a lot of comfort too.

The rest is up for grabs. Don't assume that nobody will want Popsi's dirty handkerchiefs or Nana's old hatboxes. In the wake of a departure, sentiment usually trumps taste! I've also heard of having an open house for friends and family to sift through the deceased's closet or bedroom. No matter what your role is, dealing with tangible items helps you deal with your emotions, and that's a good thing. There's nothing wrong with associating physical things with the people who wore, owned, and coveted them; it means a lot that it was theirs and you have the chance to keep a part of them with you.

If you are not in control of the doling out, and hoping to receive a token, speak up for yourself. Spirit says there's no harm in mentioning the keychain or watch you'd like, to the tune of "I loved the way Grandma looked in her polka dot sweater. When the time comes, I would like to have it if nobody minds." The alternative is remorse, though Spirit asks that you have perspective. Once I read a girl at a show in Springfield, Missouri, who lost her mother. She was hoping for her mom's wedding ring, but another family member claimed it. Even so, Spirit made me feel like she had something more special than the ring. "She wants me to tell you that even though you don't have a lot of her physical items," I said, "and that in fact other family members took them from you, they can't steal the bond and memories you shared with her. What you had together is what's truly important and worth holding on to."

Racing Against the Clock or Dragging Your Feet?

If possible, try to use foresight when deciding when to handle your loved one's items. You don't want to save too much or too little because you acted hastily to check this duty off your list. Ideally, you'll leave room to laugh, cry, or reminisce as you go, and you can only do this when you don't feel pressured. Start by thinking about how it might feel to begin sorting now or later, alone or with a friend, a little at a time or all at once. The only way for this to feel satisfying is if it's done on your watch, in your way.

Of course, you may not have a choice about how to proceed if outside forces and logistics are involved, and that's fine too. I even know a woman whose husband died from cancer, and the couple sorted his things together before he passed; this way, she could just execute when he died, and it would be one less stress amid the emotional frenzy of planning a funeral and settling an estate. Even if you're racing against the clock, Spirit says to find the silver lining to prevent regrets. Like if you need to act quickly to sell a house or clean out a room in a nursing home, maybe this inspires you to give more away than you would have otherwise. A fast turnaround could also inspire you to go all Marie Kondo without looking back, or force you to be more systematic than usual. Just be sure to ask for help, whether from an organized, decisive friend or a consignment shop that can haul away the excess and make your life easier.

If time isn't on your side, you can always make big decisions later. Consider boxing up the undecided goods, putting them in storage, and labeling it "sentimentally hoarded." You'll get to it when the time is right—next week, next month, or in a year. And if you have a few straggling items that you don't know what to do with? Follow my mom's lead. She told me that when Gram died, she made what she calls a "memory box," which was just a container where all the undecided stuff went—things that weren't immediately useful but too personal to donate or gift. Then every once in a while, or whenever someone who cared about Gram visited, Mom will go through the box and either put more stuff to use or feel OK giving it away. Mom was able to do this only because of the distance and clarity that comes with time. Though the box once held Gram's vintage coat collection and beautiful Christmas balls, for instance, it felt right to give the coats away when our church held its annual coat drive and to tie an ornament to everyone's gift during the holidays. Another item Mom saved was a box of cards and drawings that Gram had kept; for those, Mom gradually gave them back to the person who sent or created them with a note that said, "You either made this for, or gave this to, our mom, but we thought you'd like it back knowing she loved it enough to save." This took the burden off the family, who would have felt bad throwing out these mementos, while letting others know Gram cared enough to hold on to them.

The only point at which it's unhealthy to deliberate on going through one's belongings is when it contributes to a stuck or negative mind-set. This might happen if keeping a loved one's room intact encourages you to sit on her bed, stare at the walls, and sob day after day. In other words, if their stuff keeps you from living your life—going to work, seeing family, doing nice things for yourself—then it's not ideal. That said, a lot of my clients find solace in opening a closet to find their husband's terry-cloth robe or their son's smelly football jersey staring back at them. Pretty often, the souls of kids will say, "My mom kept my room exactly the same, and it's like a museum in there with a red velvet rope you can't cross! But if that's what she needs and it isn't holding her back, it's fine with me." If this sounds like you, maybe start by cleaning the sheets, putting some clothes away, and taking the process in small, manageable steps. Just like you couldn't imagine living without the person who died but are learning to carry on, you will eventually feel OK parting with their things. Spirit says it'll feel similar to having holiday decorations up in January—you'll still love them but know it's time to put them away.

If the thought of sorting and organizing gives you a pain in the pit of your stomach, Spirit says to rest assured that when you are finished, you will feel surprisingly relieved and cleansed. Thinking about the task is more intimidating than doing it or dealing with the aftermath of an empty closet, room, or home. I know a woman named June whose brother, Kip, lived with her before he died. For June, she needed to reach a point of acceptance to have the strength to sort through his things. "I didn't touch the majority of his stuff for a very long time. I didn't need the space and so his clothes sat in the closet with the door closed, in the spare bedroom," she said. "But when I finally did it, it was fine. I gave the men in his and my family a number of things. I kept one box for myself of T-shirts that had meaning, a favorite sweater, even a sweater I hated and begged him to toss for years—suddenly I needed to have it. That bin went in the attic and I keep a handful of things in my room, like a Yankees hat I wear to the beach, a T-shirt I sleep with, and a cozy sweatshirt in my closet." June donated the rest to a clothing drive at the school where Kip used to teach. "I was less emotional doing this so late in the game, even though it worked for me," she added. "It was a massive weight, and now it's nearly done."

De-Clutter a Space, De-Clutter Your Soul

Spirit says that when you get rid of things that no longer serve a purpose, it de-clutters your emotional state. I'm not talking about the meaningful items, but everything else—a spouse's cologne on the dresser, deodorant in the medicine cabinet, a pile of pennies on the corner of the piano. It's hard to let go of these mundane things because it feels like you're letting go of a part of your loved one, and removing them from your everyday life, but you're not. It's like cleaning out your own closet to get rid of sweaters or pants that no longer fit or make sense with your lifestyle. If the last time you worked in an office was eight years and three sizes ago, why hold on to a rack of size four business suits? You wouldn't. You'd make room for pieces that fit the life you have now. Grief operates the same way. Making sense of your loved one's leftovers clears space in your heart for healing and acceptance. Whether you're letting go of old golf clubs and ratty T-shirts, or depression and regret, it's all the same. My cousin Louis did this when he came across a stack of his departed father's prayer cards. What was he going to do with them—shove them in yet another attic corner? It made him anxious to have them around. So he buried them in upstate New York, where my uncle loved to hunt. When all was said and done, he could breathe again.

If you take your loved one out of the equation, having any clutter around you is found to be unhealthy. Research shows that clutter raises stress levels and can affect your relationships, mood, and physical and mental health. Keeping one versus 937 of your son's hockey trophies will contribute to your happiness because reducing clutter helps you see what you need and don't need. You put your past in order.

Make New Things, but Keep the Old . . .

A lot of clients like to get creative by turning a loved one's item into something new. Spirit wholly supports this, no matter what you make, because the reinvented item respects the integrity of the past while reimagining it in a fresh way—what a perfect symbol for growth and learning. Most commonly, clients refashion jewelry; turn clothes into quilts, pillows, and teddy bears; and refinish old furniture or home goods that they either keep for themselves or give to a loved one. To this end, I remember reading two girls whose father died, and his soul told me they changed his wedding ring—their mother had it split in half and made into heart-shaped necklaces. They were so delicate, a perfect charm! I also think it's really clever when clients create meaningful pieces from a collection of items so they don't have too much stuff to store away. So if your sister had an extensive book collection, consider taking a few for yourself and then photograph some of the others and use them for a gallery wall in your home. Or if your grandmother owned a bunch of scarves, maybe sewing them together would make for an eclectic tablecloth. This way, you save the gist of what you love, turn it into something up-to-date, and toss what could potentially create clutter.

One of the most amazing transformation stories I've channeled was related to a family that was approached with the option to donate their deceased son's eyes. His eyes! They did, and the young man's soul stepped forward to thank his parents for making this choice. Mom broke down crying and said, "My son was so optimistic and hopeful, I wanted someone else to see life through his eyes." What an awesome concept too, to think that this man's eyes are now the much-needed gateway to *another* person's soul.

Healing Moments

Let's shift the focus away from stressing over the stuff and toward grat-itude for the stuff, OK? I'd like you to sit quietly with your feet planted and palms up, and when you feel still, thank your loved one for whatever belonging you cherish most. And if you were not given one, then thank them for one memory that means the world to you.

26

Mr. Sandman, Bring Me a Spirit

Everyone loves a good dream story—I know I do! But before I get into some juicy ones, I need to clear up a misconception that about ninety-nine percent of my fans and clients have. If you believe it too, then welcome to the club. I'm talking about how most people are under the impression that when loved ones die, they'll automatically dream of them, and that dreams are one of the first, and easiest, ways a soul can say hello. Is this the case sometimes? Sure. But for many people—and for various reasons—it just isn't true.

You know, not everyone has the ability to dream of Spirit. Dreams are like any other sign in that you can connect only if your energy is compatible with this mode of communication. In other words, some of us are energetically receptive to dreams, and others aren't. If you *are* a natural, then a sleep state makes you a captive audience because your mind is at rest. And if not? Don't worry about it. What's so great about Spirit is that if your loved ones can't reach you in a dream, they'll turn to the next best thing—other signs you can read or the dreams of family and friends who can relay their messages. If you think about why Spirit visits us at all, it's for *our* comfort—for us to see they're OK, to reassure or guide us when we need them, and to aid with healing. So if the dream thing's not working out, Spirit isn't going to dwell on or stress about it. They'll simply get to you through other means. It's not worth the trouble!

Me? I've dreamed of a loved one only once. Once! And I talk to the dead for a living! It was about five months after Gramps passed. My parents had just sold his house, and I dreamed that Gram and I were in the kitchen together. She was crying happy tears. "I'm so glad you came to see the house before another family lived in it," Gram said. I told her it made me sad because it was the end of an era, but Gram said it was time to move on. She told me she supported the decisions we'd made in her absence.

No matter what the specific message or purpose, all of Spirit's dreams are special, well intentioned, and meant to act as a reminder that the soul is at peace. Call it like it is—a rare gift!

Think Positive, Dream Positive

Spirit asks you to think positive by day and dream positive by night— for good reason. Whether you experience a visitation or another kind of dream, carrying anger or burdens related to a death like guilt, regret, or fear can cause you to misinterpret a dream's intentions. When you're feeling negative, you'll automatically believe that Spirit's presence or message has a negative overtone, and that isn't the case. For example, you might interpret a quick appearance to mean that the person's soul is mad at you or didn't want to talk to you, and chose not to stick around for long. Or if the soul doesn't try again because they don't want to further upset you, you'll think it's because they're already mad at you. None of this, of course, is what's happening, and you can see where a depressed mind can conjure dark interpretations.

When you interpret a dream with seemingly unclear details, Spirit urges you to view it from a positive POV because this is *always* their perspective too. It's like how a fan named Jean dreamed of her deceased great-grandmother, whom she called Grama Polla, a few months after she died. In her dream, Jean, who was fifteen years old at the time, was looking out the glass storm door at her parents' house when she saw Grama Polla in the front yard. Grama Polla then waved for Jean to meet her at a sprawling tree, and when she did, the soul began to playfully float around it. Jean said her great-grandmother looked exactly as she remembered—glasses, white hair, small frame, brilliant smile. And though she was trying to talk to Jean the whole time, she could only hear mumbling, and before Jean knew it, the dream turned from one of happiness to a scene that felt really scary and desperate. Jean remembers, "My heart started to hurt because I couldn't catch up, and I began to cry because I didn't know what she was saying to me." When Grama Polla noticed Jean's sorrow and confusion, she stopped abruptly—and then looked into Jean's eyes with the greatest sense of love, peace, and connection Jean's ever felt. Then the dream ended!

"The way my great-grandmother looked at me made me think she had something really important to say, yet she never came back to me after that," Jean shared. Now, had she carried any heavy feelings about her great-grandmother's passing, the curious details of this dream might have haunted her for some time. Yet while Jean always wondered if she missed out on a moving message, she opted to focus instead on the dream's uplifting tone, how happy and healthy her loved one felt, and the love in Grama Polla's expression. The dream reinforced to her that her cherished family member is carefree in Heaven. When I heard this story, Spirit showed me that she was encouraging Jean to always live as if she were a child and never forget to play. In fact, my guides sang "Ring Around the Rosie . . ." as I heard this story!

Visitations: Just Passing Through!

A visitation is a type of dream in which you see a loved one's soul—on its own or within the context of a scene or story line that may or may not make much sense. A visit is usually brief, the message is concise (if there is one), and then it's over. I've had many clients whose loved ones appeared only long enough for a hug, and then disappeared. If you do have a long interaction, this is a reflection of soul strength. It takes a lot of energy for Spirit to appear in a dream and then communicate for any length of time. During live shows, in fact, newer souls with less energy borrow from older souls in the room for this reason.

When Spirit relays a verbal message during a visitation, it can be a quick exchange, a few sentences, or a word. You might also understand the meaning of a visit or message without any language at all, since souls communicate through thought. No matter what, you'll remember the message (unlike how some dreams are spotty the next day), and it will be as clear as a bell. A fan club member named Deborah said she was eighteen years old when her father was dying of cancer. Several times during his final week alive, she was told he wouldn't make it through the night, but then he'd rally and be OK. Every evening, she went to bed not knowing what the next day would bring. "One night, I dreamed of a tunnel with bright light and beautiful music," she said. "My dad was there and said, 'Don't worry about me. I am home.' " Deborah's phone rang and woke her up—it was a call from the hospital saying Dad had passed away. At the time, Deborah had never heard of the famed tunnel of light, but she's never forgotten it since.

Dreams can also offer reassurance that Spirit knows what's happening in your life and sends all their love. A woman I know named Nicole told me that her Pop-Pop died when she was thirteen years old, and not long after, she dreamed she was at a big school dance that she'd been dreading. In Nicole's dream, she stood alone at the side of the gymnasium, and not one person asked her to awkwardly sway along to the music. Just as Nicole was beginning to feel upset, her Pop-Pop appeared out of nowhere and asked her to slow dance— and this visitation had an enormous impact on Nicole. "Even at that young age I realized, 'Wow, I'm not alone,' " she said. "It was so clear that he was telling me that he understood that going to dances and being left out really worried me. He was telling me it would be OK, and it was."

One of my favorite times that Spirit makes a cameo in dreams is when a family is growing, since they know you wish they were around to celebrate. Coming to you in a dream, then, is Spirit's way of saying they aren't missing a thing! I know a woman named Jessica who, shortly after her first son was born, told her mom that if she had another child, she'd hoped she could give her son a brother. Her mom gently disagreed. "Not me," she said. "I hope it's a girl so that I can relive all the things I did with you when you were little." Nine months later, Jessica's mom unexpectedly died from colon cancer. Jessica became pregnant shortly after, and the night of her ultrasound when she learned she was having—you guessed it—a second son, she dreamed about telling her mom the news. In her soul state, Mom was thrilled. When the baby was finally born, Jessica dreamed of her mom again. This time, she was at a pool party of all places, and her mom was there. Jessica handed her the baby and said, "This is him!" She remembers her mom's expression—calm and happy: "Mom took him in her arms. I heard her voice again. I saw her face. It was amazing in every way." Though Jessica often wondered if these dreams were truly visits from her mom's soul, I have no doubt they were. In fact, Spirit showed me that Mom came to her to assure her that while she's no longer on earth, her soul has held her son's soul; this was also an unspoken affirmation that Jessica will feel all the love, happiness, and joy that her mother felt having her as a daughter.

And because Spirit's all about support and guidance, they appear to us in dreams when we need a boost of strength and optimism. An incredible visitation happened to a friend named Kate who experienced five miscarriages, with two children born during very complicated deliveries. I mention this because as you can imagine, by the time Kate was pregnant for the *eighth* time, she was pretty stressed out. Adding to her anxiety, and in the weeks preceding her first ultrasound, Kate's thirty-seven-year-old brother had open-heart surgery and her friend's forty-year-old husband died from an undiagnosed heart condition while on a bike ride. On the night of Kate's dream, she says she was seven weeks pregnant and fell asleep thinking about heart problems. Poor thing!

"In my dream, we were visiting my brother in the hospital and my late grandfather Gil, who'd been a cardiothoracic surgeon, was there," she said, adding that he died a few months after her wedding. "He came over to me and said, 'Katie, it is so good to see you. So good to meet your family.' I knew he knew I was pregnant and scared. He looked right into my eyes, and in his deep, distinct voice said, 'Everything is going to be OK.' I knew he was right." When Kate woke up, she felt an overwhelming calm for the first time in years—plus an unexplainable sense of knowing and a flash of inspiration.

Kate woke her husband from a sound sleep to tell him what had happened. "Honey, everything is going to be OK," she said. "We're going to have a boy, and we're going to name him Gilbert." Kate said she never even settled on a girl's name, because she instinctually knew she didn't need one. Her healthy son Gilbert was born a few months later. After the dream, Kate dug up an old key tag from her grandfather's medical school locker that her parents had engraved with Kate's initials after he died. At the time, she thought it was cool but didn't wear it very often. "But after my son Gilbert's birth, it became the most precious piece of jewelry I own—more precious than my wedding ring. I actually lost my diamond wedding ring while skiing, and my husband and I gave up looking for it and drank a beer, toasting the fact that our marriage outlasted the ring! But if I lost that necklace, I'd be *devastated*."

Dreams That Make You Go *Hmmm*

Spirit can also visit you within a dream that's long, rambling, and creative—a jumble of thoughts, images, and feelings that warrant a little interpretation. These dreams might also reflect any emotions, wishes, or activities that happened during the day. Listen, you might not even remember anything else from the dream—nothing may even make sense—but if Spirit's presence is visitation-like, consider it their soul saying hi. Now, some mediums like to draw a hard line between dreams and visitations, but it's not a black-and-white issue for me. Sometimes a visitation in the context of a dream is just proof that the soul is alive and aware that you're thinking of them, that they're part of your greater life and consciousness.

A great example of a clear visitation within the context of a non-sensical dream came from a fan named Leslie, who dreamed of her Gramps shortly after he passed. He was her best friend while he was alive and she still prays to him all the time. Leslie dreamed she was driving down the road and saw Gramps standing on the shoulder, near a junkyard! She picked him up; he climbed into the backseat and began giving her directions. Because Leslie was no longer navigating the road, she remembers feeling lost and not knowing where she was headed—yet his soul kept saying, "It's OK. Trust me." Once Leslie acquiesced, the car stopped and Gramps was now outside the car, on the other side of the driver's-side window with Leslie at the steering wheel. Then it was over. When I heard this dream, Spirit showed me this was Gramps's way of saying, "I hear all of your prayers, and I am still loving, guiding, and listening to you. So when you feel alone and lost, know that I am right beside you to help you find your way."

Going Through Others to Get to You

If you don't connect to dreams, Spirit may appear to another person and urge them to tell you about it. This can happen if you're having a hard time seeing signs or if Spirit feels you're too sad or distracted to interpret a visitation in a positive way. Your loved ones might also feel that going through another person will strengthen your relationship with the dreamer or allow that person to support you when they didn't previously know how. Clearly Spirit is looking out and will use every trick in the book to prove it!

During a live show in Jacksonville, I read a woman named Lidija who'd flown all the way from Croatia to attend the event. Yes, Croatia—that's fourteen thousand miles away! After her son Marko died at thirty-one years old in a motorcycle accident while out with friends, she began reading about me online and talking to her sister in Miami about what she found. With each click and conversation, she says she felt her "son's love" leading her to me. So Lidija enrolled in my fan club and on her son's birthday, after watching my TV show, she called her sister and told her to get tickets. As these things go, Lidija was one of the first people I noticed from the stage, and her son's soul made every second of her trip worthwhile.

What I love about Lidija's unique story isn't that she has intimate dreams of Marko, but that *his best friend* from childhood named Ado does! In fact, Ado says he's had over one hundred (!) of them— and every few weeks, he calls Lidija to share her son's messages from Heaven. These are often related to events that either happen a day before or after the dream. Once when Lidija and her husband were arguing, Ado dreamed that Marko told him that he finds it upsetting that his parents aren't more loving with each other. And another time, Lidija went to the ER for anxiety and chest pain late at night. That same evening, Ado—without knowing that Lidija had been in the hospital—told her that Marko came to him in a dream and said, "My mom isn't well—she's sick over my death. Go immediately to her and tell her I'm OK. Tell her that every evening, I stand next to her and kiss her on the cheek, though she doesn't know it." Lidija is beyond touched that Marko loves her so much that he stays close through his friend, and because of his messages, Lidija and Ado have discovered a new bond.

Healing Moments

I don't want you to rely on your dreams to help you have a good or bad day. As with anything in life—religion, politics, even health—I think it is unwise to seek out only one source of happiness or guidance. So if you dream of Spirit, I'd like you to keep your journal by your bedside, along with a flashlight, and record your dreams so that you have them in writing to reread when you wake up. If, on the other hand, you want to dream but can't, I want you to try something else. Don't put so much pressure on yourself and Spirit before bed. Thank your loved ones for showing you signs, for watching over and guiding you, and then say, "Thank you for coming in a dream when you're ready." Have faith and put the request in Spirit's hands. I can't tell you the number of times clients swear they don't dream of a loved one, then once they open up to Spirit a bit more, they dream like crazy. You never know!

27

Laugh Like You Mean It

Spirit always says laughter is the best medicine for the soul—
which is more truth than cliché, trust me. This is because laughter is
healing and restorative, and whether you giggle or guffaw, your energy
changes for the better. In fact, if you pay attention, you can actually
feel your energy, or vibration, shift as it lightens and brightens. You
know how you feel cleansed and rejuvenated after a good belly laugh?
Like you've just washed your soul out with Listerine? That's the feeling
of a raised vibration. Or have you ever noticed that when you watch
a funny show or skit—like for me, it's James Corden's "Carpool Kara-
oke" on *The Late Late Show*—you can feel chills shimmy through your
whole body? That's because you're receiving positive energy. It's also
you sensing your loved one who's laughing right beside you. Never
doubt that Spirit loves a good reason to chuckle. They don't stop having fun just because they're dead!

In case you're wondering (and I know you are), it is completely
appropriate to laugh when you're grieving. Light comedy, dark humor,
big laughs, small snickers—it's all good. In fact, it's necessary.

Laugh, and Spirit Laughs with You

Spirit says that when we grieve, we tend to forget how to laugh. This is one of the reasons I ask souls to keep it light when I channel them and to communicate with humor and personality. So sometimes Spirit will have me curse to bring up the mood in the room or do crazy things to demonstrate how someone's brother or spouse acted or spoke. At a show in Brooklyn, I had a badass soul that kept encouraging me to eat M&M's that had fallen to the floor—for no real rhyme or reason, except that it was a funny dare. It makes us laugh to remember personality quirks like this and helps the soul come alive before our eyes.

When Spirit tells "remember when" stories to validate that it's truly your loved ones speaking to you, they love to tell stories that will make you laugh. They do this to feed your soul, raise your energy, and help you with your healing so that you can start embracing life without them. I remember doing a show where a young man in the audience had lost his brother unexpectedly; his mom was there as well. The soul told me that he wanted to talk about the brother's tattoo that nobody knows about. At this point, the mother looked at her son and said "You have a tattoo?" and sure enough, he lifted up his shirt and on the back of his neck was a tattoo in memory of his brother! As if this didn't put the guy in enough hot water with his mom, the soul upped his game. "Ask my brother about the underwear too," he said. So here I am, thinking the young man's going to say he's wearing his brother's old underwear or not wearing any at all, and instead he said, "Well, this is the story. My friends threw me a surprise party for my birthday, and we ended up, um, in a strip club. They called me onstage and cut off my underwear!" Secrets, strip club, public nudity—at this point, the mother is *dying*. She even sat down from embarrassment, and I'm not gonna lie, she looked a little upset. When I noticed this, the soul confessed, "I know I'm causing trouble, but I haven't seen my brother laugh like that since the day I died"—and in that moment, I knew that laughter was Spirit's big motivation all along. This jokester knew how important it was to make his brother laugh again, even at the cost of throwing off Mom. Hearing personal, hilarious stories from his brother's soul also assured him that there's an afterlife, that he is safe and happy, and it softened his heart to receive healing. These tales put him in the right mind-set to do the work he needed to do next—forgive, let go of anger, move past guilt, whatever it was—to carry on with his life.

Spirit, by nature, is very playful. Your loved ones' souls are made of light, and they have no reason to feel anything *but* bliss and good vibes in Heaven. Little kids, in fact, tug at my skirt or pants, because their souls are so lively and lighthearted. I also remember channeling a husband whose shtick was to always make his wife laugh, and this drive didn't stop when he crossed over. At first, he came through with mushy validations—he knows about the tree she planted, that she speaks to his soul at night, that she shares stories of how they first met . . . But after a while he said, "How long do I have to be serious, Theresa? Can I say something funny?"—which was so him! Spirit can also turn on the charm for a smile, as was the case with a teenage boy who died. His whole gang showed up for the reading—Mom, Dad, his brother, and four friends. At one point, the soul grabbed my butt (oh, yes he did); I felt like I'd been touched, and then a warm sensation spread through my rear. I was so shocked, I shouted, "Hey, you can't do that!" and the soul's friends, not knowing what happened, were dying. "Is he flirting with you?" asked one guy. "Because he would think you're totally hot—you're his type!" The audience burst out laughing, and just like that, the energy of every suffering person in there shot through the roof.

Don't Wait for Laughter to Find You

When we laugh, it reminds our souls that we can, and will, feel OK again—but depending on the day, it might take some effort. Some days, you need to give yourself permission to allow joy to shine through the darkness, and on others, you might have to actively find reasons to laugh. It's not always enough to wait for a funny moment to come knocking, especially if you aren't going out as much. It's also not rude or disrespectful to the person who died to have your funny bone tickled. The only thing I ask is that when you're looking for ways to smile, don't put absurd expectations on how incredibly awesome you'll feel by, say, watching an *Ellen* clip on YouTube or old iPhone videos of your niece. Spirit says that just because laughter is the opposite of crying, a good giggle doesn't make *all* your grief disappear. The win is in knowing that you've found a break in the clouds, which you now know exists and can happen again.

It's nice to find ways to connect laughter to your loved one's memory too. Spirit suggests calling a friend or family member who told the kookiest stories at the funeral and asking that person to call or send you an email with any others if they think of them. You could also email close confidants to ask them to share their most amusing moments with your loved one in an email chain. The more you laugh, the easier it will be to laugh again and again. Think of humor as a muscle that you need in order to go through life but that without exercise will atrophy. You must stretch, flex, and lean on it. Use it or lose it, baby!

Sometimes the easiest way to laugh is to surround yourself with cheerful, easygoing people. Whether that means sitting in the audience at an improv show or grabbing lunch with a witty friend, their good humor is bound to rub off on you. Hey, science backs me up on this. Studies show that when you laugh in the company of others, there's a real, contagious response happening. Think about how, when you walk into a room where two people are laughing—but you never heard what started it—you crack a smile automatically. Researchers say this is because the brain responds to the sound of laughter by prepping the muscles in the face to mimic the sound and then grin or laugh. What's even crazier is that when subjects in one university study listened to negative versus positive sounds, the brain had a stronger reaction to the positive sounds, suggesting that they're more contagious than the negative ones! No wonder you're more prone to laugh along to a laugh track on a sitcom but you wouldn't necessarily frown when, say, a person gags. In other words, your brain wants to *be* happy and your body wants to *express* it!

Above all, laughter is proof that there are reasons to feel glad when you are ready to see them—that the world isn't only bad and that the universe gives us sunny moments to offset the tragic ones. The elation that occurs when you're caught up in a cheerful moment can be life-changing. Did you ever catch the viral video about how friends and family honored a man named Ger "Farmer" Foley, who passed from cystic fibrosis? If not, you *have* to google it. After Ger's funeral, friends and family raised a pint to him in an Irish pub, and then his friend Brian led the crowd in the most lively, passionate, and heartfelt rendition of the Killers' song "Mr. Brightside" that I've ever heard! Singing in one's honor is customary at Irish wakes, but this really took the wake cake! In the video, Brian stomps his feet, claps his hands, pounds on his heart, and then tears off his shirt and flings it into the crowd. You can see how the group is laughing, crying, and jumping up and down with fists pumping in the air. Everyone turns so red in the face that I was worried their hearts would explode from all that emotion! What's so moving isn't just that this raucous concert is a celebration of Ger's life, but a moment in *everyone's* life that's filled with laughter, love, and positivity. It's an absolutely perfect tribute and emotional release all rolled into one.

Healing Moments

I like reading famous quotes about laughter that remind me of how global this need is. For example, Quincy Jones said, "I've always thought that a big laugh is a really loud noise from the soul saying, 'Ain't that the truth.' " And Bob Hope: "I have seen what a laugh can do. It can transform almost unbearable tears into something bearable, even hopeful." And Milton Berle: "Laughter is an instant vacation." This last one really hits home for me when I think about grief, because when you laugh, you're momentarily transported to a kinder, gentler, emotional place within yourself. It's not a spot where your troubles don't exist at all; they just get a much-needed break, complete with sunshine, breezes, and a piña colada or two.

For this activity, I want you to find a quote that makes you laugh or is about laughter and write it on a notecard. You can do this plainly with a pen or have some fun—use colorful markers, your child's stickers, cut pictures from magazines, and make it pretty or silly or relevant to your life so that you feel happy looking at it. Then tape the card where you can't miss it, like on your fridge or bathroom mirror. This will remind you to smile or laugh at some point every day.

28

You *Can* Handle the Truth!

When I hear grief experts use the term "acceptance," I tend to take pause. The popular meaning is that you're acknowledging your loved one is gone in a permanent way, and while you might not like it, you've learned to live with it. I mean . . . yes and no. Spirit says that true acceptance, in both spiritual and practical terms, is about fully recognizing that while your loved ones are no longer in their physical body, they are with you in soul-form and able to connect in various ways. It means going through life as capable, confident, and optimistic as you can be about managing the future. It involves trusting that your separation is temporary until you see each other in Heaven. Acceptance is knowing that your loved one is at peace and though you're left to finish this life without them, you're relatively at peace with that too.

Spirit's definition of acceptance is also terrifically proactive. It's not just a state of mind, but an intention to get moving with the universe's help. It's like the gates of Heaven have flown open and God, loved ones, and other Spirit have been finally freed to help you make the rest of your life a win. Their attention is no longer focused on getting you through sorrow but showing you opportunities for joy and fulfillment. And if grief unexpectedly comes knocking? No worries. They'll guide you back to your path so that you can continue to color in the promising details of your new normal.

Gaining Perspective with Loss

A lot of my clients assume that our ability to deal with a departure exists on a relative scale corresponding to the details of the death. Like, you might believe that whether a person was old or if a departure happened suddenly, this would impact how tough it is to find peace. But Spirit says that's not how it works. A loss is a loss—one recovery isn't easier than another—and the grief process is too multi-layered for a one-size-fits-all response. A huge misunderstanding, for instance, is that acceptance is easier to come by if you lose a spouse but have kids. Yet one woman might have a harder time because she's terrified of being a single mom while another might do a little better because her kids keep her busy and force her to put on a brave face.

When you accept a passing, a healthy perspective follows. Yes, you've lost a loved one but you realize that good things can come from it. Maybe it's that the person isn't suffering anymore or that their death left you a robust inheritance that lets you chase your dreams without feeling financially hamstrung. Listen, this is progress! If you remember back to when your loved one first died, it was all a catastrophe—you were caught in a whirlwind of despair and chaos, and the sky was falling everywhere you looked. Grief has also taught you lessons about wisdom and compassion because you know what it is to suffer and come out the other side. You've become a more sympathetic human being, as God intended.

Accepting loss, then, is about welcoming change. Incredible proof is a woman I read in Brooklyn, who met her future husband at her fiancé's funeral. The men were close friends! Sadly, the fiancé committed suicide and came through to say, "Thank you for loving her like I couldn't and giving her the life I never did." His soul told me he was always troubled and his fiancée was too kind to leave. So in this case, change came with a blessing—it brought a couple together to enjoy a loving relationship. The thing about change is that we let it scare us and probably shouldn't, because we can change for the better. It's like how a woman named Molly, who, upon getting married, moved from Manhattan to the Jersey suburbs to be with her spouse. She loved their life but always thought wistfully about the time she spent in the city. When her husband died, it took Molly years to consider moving back, but she eventually found that heading to New York again helped her find her groove among the people and places she loved so much. Talking about this, Spirit made me feel Molly's soul come alive—an exciting rebirth from a traumatic setback.

The Limits of Acceptance

When you're in a state of acceptance, you can hear back-to-back radio songs that speak to you, smile at the owl sent from your loved one, and meditate until you're blue in the face—in other words, embrace that soul bond for all it's worth—but it will *never* feel the same as having your loved one beside you in a physical form. I don't for one second want you to think I'm saying that the two scenarios should bring out identical feelings in you, because they are incredibly different. This is why clients, especially spiritual ones, get stuck indefinitely, because they believe it's going to feel the same or even more amazing to have a relationship with Spirit. But acceptance isn't self-delusion. On good days, you will feel supremely comforted and connected; on bad days, it'll seem like a nice consolation prize. That's just how it is.

Because we most noticeably miss our loved ones when activities and events roll around, Spirit says acceptance may need to come one milestone at a time. It's one thing to mentally accept that a person died and something else to feel OK that they won't walk you down the aisle at your wedding, pick up the phone when you call, or be there for the birth of your child. The more you feel their souls with you during these times, the more accepting you'll be of this change—but you won't ever stop wishing things were different. Like for me, I've accepted and embraced that Gram and Gramps died and are in Heaven, and I know I'll see them again, but there are still times I drive past their street and think, *I wish I could just drop by for a cup of coffee and stay for a half hour; it made us so happy.* These kinds of thoughts and daily reminders will always be a part of your life no matter how at peace you feel. The counselors, then, are right when they take it a step further and say that just because you're at peace doesn't mean you have to like what happened. Even so, Spirit says to hold on to the fact that the questions that used to play on your mind—*Did you make the right choices? Could you have prevented the death? Are they with God?*—are usually much quieter during acceptance, no matter how much you still hate that your loved one has died. You may even sense positive answers or have let the questions go, which shows remarkable growth.

Healing Moments

Before you go to bed tonight, take five minutes to think about the positive changes that have come from your loved one's passing. In no way will these make you *glad* that your loved one only exists in spirit, but they should feel like blessings that help compensate for the pain you've felt thus far. I'm thinking a new pet, new friends, and fresh priorities like eating well or taking time to read . . . What's on your list?

29

Search Your Soul

If you can't stop thinking about how your life and God's intentions square up, welcome to the upside of grieving. It forces you to slow down, think about your circumstances, consider what it will take to feel happy, and then build yourself up from this point—in other words, soul search. After all this, you owe it to yourself to figure out what puts a skip in your step every day. Use this time to consider, *What is it that I still like about my life that fulfills my soul, and what needs to go? What else will it take to feel like a positive version of myself again?* Maybe you'll realize you want to spend more time with family and exercise more, so you move your work hours to part-time and sign up for tennis lessons. Death strips us bare, so use your most honest state to take a good look at who you are and act on what you see and feel.

Spirit likes a tactical approach to soul-searching, so try to do what it takes to emerge from your reflections feeling lighter and more determined to love yourself and have a more positive influence on those who also struggle. Really believe that God hasn't singled you out for a miserable journey but to learn from the hand you've been dealt. Become living proof that life should be embraced, not simply endured.

Don't Ask, Unless You're Willing to Listen

When you're depressed, it's normal to question everything, but you must pause to really listen for answers. If you quiet yourself long enough to tune into your instincts and notice the opportunities around you, you'll realize that there is hope and that Spirit guides you in this way. The thing I don't want you to do is put a ton of pressure on yourself to unearth enormous, brilliant epiphanies during such quiet time. *Go easy*. Soul-searching is hard enough when your heart is in one piece!

I'm always in awe of what happens when clients combine amazing contemplation with inner strength: They not only turn around their own situation, but also change the hearts and minds of others. Years ago, I read a family whose youngest daughter, Brianna, died, at eleven years old, when an oncoming boat struck theirs just off Fire Island in New York. Brianna suffered massive trauma to her head and torso, and her parents, Gina and Frank, also had severe head and facial injuries from the accident. Gina and her older daughter, Danyelle, had tried to resuscitate Brianna, with Danyelle administering CPR to no avail.

For years after, Danyelle suffered from depression, as did Gina, who was also very angry and felt stuck between two worlds. "I wanted so badly to be with Brianna in Heaven, and I ached for that, but on the other hand, I still had my daughter Danyelle to take care of," Gina told me. "Danyelle deserved to have a mother to talk, listen, hang out, and be silly with. I had a lot of guilt—I felt I should have been able to protect Brianna from dying. I asked God every day to take me. There were many days I didn't even come out of my room—consumed by tears and sleeplessness—trying to shut out the world around me."

When I channeled Brianna during a private reading, her soul came through to specifically help Gina move forward. Brianna helped Gina realize that she wants her mom to live as if she were still alive, and made Gina see that she had some soul-searching to do to figure out how to put one foot in front of the other. To this end, she'd find herself thinking about what would make her happy and honor her daughter—this, while driving, meditating, cooking, or at any other moment she could find to quiet her mind. Ultimately, Gina realized that going back to work, opening a business, and dedicating more time to Danyelle would give her a sense of purpose and calm her restlessness. "I realized how short life is and that it was possible to move forward," she said. Doing tremendous good in Brianna's honor has also been a salve to her emotional state. Gina's fought to change boating laws to help save lives and opened an indoor sporting facility in Brianna's memory called Breezy's Field of Dreams (Breezy was Brianna's nickname). Her family's donated many scholarships to high school students and gives back to their community by collecting toys and Easter baskets for underprivileged children in the area. "By returning to life full force, I am a better person," she said. "I believe you should take your pain and turn it into something positive, be there for those who need you, and know it's possible to have a better tomorrow. I could take these steps only after many hours of asking my soul what it needed to go on. I now know it's OK to be busy, laugh, and no longer feel angry at God." Danyelle too has become incredibly resilient. I recently saw her speak at a balloon-release ceremony for her sister, and I was so impressed with how mature and poised she'd become. Though you can't change that a person has passed, or the details around that event, Gina's family is proof that you *can* alter how you feel about it and how you live with that experience.

Spirit says your ultimate goal with soul-searching is acceptance— and not just acceptance that your loved one died or is at peace. They want you to accept yourself and your new place in this world. It takes an open mind and eager soul to evaluate life's unfolding and look for the means to improve it.

Give Yourself Some Love

Spirit hopes that as you do your soul-searching you won't just learn how to put one foot in front of the other, but also how to love and feel proud of yourself as you do. You know, I've noticed that a strange thing happens when we grieve. On the one hand, your grief causes you to put yourself at the center of your universe—where nobody else's feelings matter as much as yours and nobody mourns as hard as you do—but on the other hand, you don't value your needs or who you are in a positive way, like most people who put themselves at the center of their universe! Isn't that something? Instead, you hold yourself accountable for situations you can't control, beat yourself up for choices that seemed good at the time, and second-guess relationships that wouldn't have crossed your mind to doubt otherwise. So as you soul-search, Spirit needs for you to change *how* you're concentrating on yourself. They want you to focus on appreciating who you are and recognizing your gifts. They want you to use what you learn to make your life, and the lives of others, better.

I've always thought that the phrase "love yourself" looks good on a pillow, but I don't think a lot of people know how to execute this in real life. Spirit says it's not that tough—loving yourself is about replacing self-critical thoughts, words, and emotions with a more positive perspective. It's taking care of yourself when you grieve, from eating well to asking for what you need. Loving yourself also means respecting your great and not-so-great traits so that you can flesh out who you are and recognize how you should grow (by, say, admitting you have outstanding compassion for friends but you really should spend more time helping out your parents). Loving yourself also means doing what makes *you* happy. You might come to realize that life's too short not to learn how to ride horses or that it's time to explore your belief system more deeply and find a new place of worship. During grief and beyond, your goal is to appreciate and feed what makes your soul thrive. You are responsible for that. You *choose* that.

If it sounds hard to shift from a despondent headspace to one of self-love—to try to think of yourself in any other context besides that of feeling sad and lonely—Spirit says to start by reflecting on awesome conversations and memories you shared with your deceased loved ones. So first, think of a time that felt good and made you feel confident, appreciated, loved, or whatever positive feelings come to mind. Then, think about which of your qualities helped those good times occur. So for example, if you like remembering how your late aunt smiled when you covered her with a soft fur blanket at the hospital, applaud yourself not just for your kindness and good taste but also for knowing she'd feel more like "herself" if she kept warm this way. Or let's say it makes your heart happy to think how you slept next to your niece when she was sick, even though you had an early meeting the next day; appreciate, then, how generously you tend to put the needs of others first. The compassion, drive, spontaneity, or humor that make those memories so valuable is what makes *you* valuable. And if these characteristics improved your loved one's quality of life, you better believe you're meant to keep using them! Honoring the most outstanding traits you put into the world builds your self-esteem and nourishes the soul. You become a better person and appreciate who you deserve to be.

Healing Moments

I have a friend whose high school English teacher used to say, "At the end of the day, if you did your best, then it was a good day." Don't you just love that? Every once in a while, I want you to take a beat and ask yourself, *Was I the best person I could be today?*—then reflect on what you did that was great and who you were in those actions. Spirit says it's easy to forget the things we do that are good when we're so caught up in how we could have done more or been better. Let's change that!

30

The New-ish You

At some point soon, if it hasn't happened already, you will come to the gentle realization that you're having more good days than bad. That's amazing! Your positive intentions and enthusiasms are taking precedence, and as a result, your life looks pretty different. For one, you're doing some of the activities you pursued before your loved one died—maybe you want to be around nature again or you're thinking about a vacation to have some fun rather than run away from your blues. You're also open to new relationships and you initiate outings rather than wait for the phone to ring. On a deeper level, you've learned about what feeds your soul, which makes you eager to tell others and put it to good use. Though it came at a price, loss has given you a deeper relationship with yourself. I hope you can see the beauty in that.

The more you continue to soul-search, feel comfortable in your new normal, and discover meaningful ways to feel happiness, the more your sadness will level out. Grief will always be a hand on your shoulder, but not always such a heavy one. Soon you'll feel ready to begin your next chapter, and don't worry if you aren't sure what that means for you. Your soul and Spirit already have a few ideas.

"Now What?" Déjà Vus

The first time you asked "So, now what?" you were drowning in a sea of change just after a loved one's departure. Now you're ready to wade into uncharted waters again—and this time by choice! Clients tell me it's hard to figure out what to go after first, and how, when they finally feel ready to make some changes. Is it a new job or a move? Should you start dating again or have another baby? Maybe just throw a bunch of options against the wall and see what sticks?

You're in a big healing moment right now, so try not to treat your next steps too lightly. First, Spirit says to think about what you need to *feel* most, and use those feelings as a guide for how to come up with your next steps. Your emotions are the perfect navigational tool here, since as you've learned, our souls communicate with us through our feelings; if you listen to them, this is your best shot at acting in tandem with Spirit. So do you need to feel professional? Desirable? Independent? Funny? Make sure the changes you're kicking around will solicit these emotions and then create a to-do list that makes you feel inspired. If above all you need to feel confident and self-assured again, and you think a weekly trapeze class will bring that out in you, maybe this plan comes first. If independence is next in line, and going to the movies alone will make you feel self-sufficient, do that second. If feeling accomplished is your next priority, take a class that will open doors to a cool new hobby. And so on. Connecting activities with the emotions they provoke will also help you really hone in on what you desire—and what you don't. Like if I read somewhere that a bubble bath is really calming after a long, hard day, but the emotion it conjures in me is "Yuck—too wrinkly," that's not the response I'd be going for! But if I wrote down "soothed and happy" because the bubbles might make me feel moisturized and relaxed, and I'm dying to just shut off my head and dive into a self-loving soak, it's a great choice. You with me on this?

Your future goals, of course, are going to include fun *and* serious activities that fill your soul. Spirit says that when choosing these, it may help to not only see yourself as the person you were before the loss but also as the person you've since become (which includes prior aspects of your identity, but isn't the whole enchilada anymore). Like you may have always thought it'd be great to open a candy shop one day, but now the thought of peddling Swedish fish feels silly—or maybe it resonates even more because you lost a child or your loved one had a sweet tooth and you want to do this in their honor. Either way, it's OK that you've changed. Own it! It might also help to take a look at what brought you the most happiness and positivity in your mind, body, and/or soul while you've been grieving—and if it still has a positive place in your life, consider pursuing it in a new way. Take a reflexology class if a weekly foot massage was really healing and you'd like to help others feel similarly cared for, or if journaling brought you peace, take a writing class and aim to get an article published in a magazine or newspaper.

Though you don't technically have a new life, you'll see yours through a new lens. Not to trivialize things, but it reminds me of when I used to go on vacation with the kids. We'd always do what they wanted, and so to me, exploring the country meant discovering the best amusement parks, tastiest pizza spots, and cleanest public toilets. Now that the kids are older and I travel for work or with my husband, Larry, I see the world in a new way. I'm interested in museums, shops, and restaurants without chicken fingers! So your life is still your life, but now there may be time to go to a lecture series moderated by a favorite author or sign up for a spirituality workshop. Just be sure to do what you do because it enriches who you are and *not* to kill time or because your counselor thinks you'd like it. You're beyond that!

Can Your Loved Ones Help Out?

You can one hundred percent ask your loved ones to guide you to relationships and opportunities for growth, but don't ignore *your* role in this too. Spirit will only steer you, not do things for you, and there's also something wonderful about feeling capable to do and own the work yourself right now. I suggest one of two routes. I like to put my overarching desire out into the universe—for instance, to feel less stressed, more content, peaceful, joyful, loved, and relaxed—and then look for the opportunities Spirit sends that fit the bill. Or, I get really specific about what I need but thank God for providing it before I get it ("Thank you for guiding me to where I should look for a job and for placing prospects in my path. I ask that I will instinctively know when it's right"). Then I do my part, and you should do yours—contact headhunters, call a real estate agent, sign up for Match.com . . . Help Spirit help you. Know too that while late Aunt Ginny doesn't play favorites—it's not like she'll help you get a job but not a date— Spirit can only do so much since you're meant to use your free will to evaluate and make good choices. I know, it'd be so much easier if God contracted a fleet of angels to do the dirty work for us, but that's not how it goes. They'll guide, but follow-through is on you.

We are on this plane to grow, learn, and thrive, so please, be an active participant in your own life again. Spirit and I can't emphasize this point enough. You can't say that you want to start going to parties because it'll make you feel social again, and then stay home when you receive an invitation to a Halloween party because you don't feel like dressing up! You have to commit to moving forward. Know that the first few opportunities you're shown might not be perfect, but they'll act as training wheels for what comes later. God doesn't always bring you the best possibility on the first go, or He may and you might not recognize it. Don't ask me why this happens, but it likely has something to do with learning lessons.

Slurp Up the Energy

One of the enormous benefits of adding a joyful and purposeful layer to your new normal is that it puts you in like-minded company where you can absorb nourishing energy. As you know, we all give off energy and have the potential to thrive off each other too. This universal law reminds me of the saying "You are what you eat." Spirit says you are who you choose to be around—that is, the energy you ingest informs the person you become. If I'm in a bad mood but then spend time with my cousin Lisa cracking jokes, I forget what made me sad in the first place. And if I'm in a great mood and then happen to, say, sit next to a Debbie Downer on the airplane, I'm definitely going to crave a stiff drink and a nap when we land.

When college kids head into their first jobs, or people with chronic illness need a survivor to inspire them, they often find a mentor or role model who gives them guidance by way of example. I think this is a great idea for stepping into *your* next chapter too. For me, I admire the way my mother grieves a passing but carries on. She takes time to feel sad yet is also respectful about the fact that everyone heals in their own time. She continues to do what needs to get done in her everyday life, yet the energy behind it is never dismissive or overly perfunctory. Mom credits her strong faith for most of this. Even before we knew I could talk to the dead, she believed in Heaven and felt deceased loved ones are with us constantly. So when Gram and Gramps died, she made their souls part of her ongoing life—and it kept her life going.

Consequently, Mom segued from grief to healing in a natural way. She visited the cemetery on a regular basis, not to be with her loved ones' souls, but to do what she calls "maintain the property"—put out flowers for holidays and keep the area around their tombstones nice. "I feel like we go together to see their property," she said. "I know they aren't at the cemetery waiting for me." Mom also talks to Spirit as part of her daily life. When Gram passed and Mom had to help move things around to make Gramps's living area more comfortable, Mom tidied up while saying in her mind, "Mom, I am not ready for this, but I want to make it safe for Dad." And when she visited Gramps, who lived alone for a few years, she'd straighten up, like wash the curtains or clean up the kitchen while quietly thinking, "I'm doing this for you, Mom." I actually didn't know Mom did this until one day Gram's soul came to me while Gramps was still alive and said, "Please thank your Mom for everything she does for me"—and Mom had to explain what she meant! And while Mom still cries all the time, she makes her next moves—whether it's deciding what to do with Gram's house or what class to take for fun—knowing she has her parents' presence and support every step of the way. "I know they haven't gone anywhere, except out of my sight," she said.

Healing Moments

In your journal, make a to-do list like the one we talked about earlier, pairing the emotions you need to feel right now with the activities you suspect will create them. If you want to get creative, you can colorfully doodle all around the list or cut out images from a magazine to make this page as inspiring as it can be! After all, we're talking about your future here. What does your soul have in store for you?

31

From Grief to Gratitude

If you can't tell, my mom is chock full of wisdom. She's been around the grief block—not just with Gram and Gramps, but from helping friends, family, and those she's advised as a bereavement counselor at our church. And one of Mom's pearls is that she compares the grief process to a spiral—an *upward* spiral, that is, not a downward one. I love this image because it makes me think of the grand staircases you see on those mansion tours in Newport, Rhode Island. Have you been? Oh, you have to go. They're insane.

Anyway, so Mom says that when you grieve, your aim is to reach the top part of the spiral, which is where your new normal exists. Climbing those stairs takes work—you break a sweat, your muscles ache, and you can't stop wondering, *Does this damn thing go on forever?* Once in a while, you might need to rest and catch your breath before carrying on, and when a wave of sadness comes on suddenly and rushes toward you like a crowd of tourists with no manners, you might even be forced to take a few steps back to let the chaos pass. Even so, you never retreat so much that you're at the bottom of the stairs where you began. You might *feel* that way at first, but if you truly do look back, you'll see how far you've come.

At the very top of the spiral staircase is gratitude—being able to recognize the good stuff around you and thanking a higher power or Spirit for their role in its creation. Appreciation is imperative to the universe and at the apex of your grief process because it generates an incredible amount of positive energy. It's a sign of healing, because you can't be stuck in grief and at the same time notice there's a whole world that exists outside your inner state. Right? One of the things I love most about gratitude is that because we're human and bad stuff happens, we don't always have it in us to shove our most positive foot forward. Gratitude, then, is the simplest way to lift yourself and others no matter what you woke up feeling. It's the best way to keep your energy high and light, which helps you embrace life every day.

You've Come a Long Way, Baby

The fact that you can feel, and just wrap your head around, the concept of appreciation is an *enormous* healing milestone—you know what I mean? When your loved one first died, you weren't able to see outside yourself or beyond your grief to admit that anything positive might exist at all. If I had mentioned gratitude at the start of this book, you might have slammed it shut and thought, *OK, whatever, Theresa. You want me to be thankful right now? For what—the fact that I don't get out of bed all day? That I feel like my heart's been torn into a million pieces and my life is an upside-down mess? Seriously, lady? Zip it.*

But now—now!—you wouldn't dare say those kinds of impetuous, nasty words to me or anyone else who tries to help you (I hope!). Instead, you can see the point to feeling glad for the details of your life that make you smile, and you understand how they benefit you. The actual moments for which you feel grateful don't have to be super deep or meaningful. Just feeling thankful for a blue sky, your child's bear hugs, or your mom's gnocchi Bolognese gives your mind and energy a major boost.

Spirit says the more you feel gratitude, the more you'll want to express it. Grief can feel isolating and lonely, a little selfish even, so enjoy how it feels to naturally want to contribute to someone else's happiness. It's a simple and wonderful gift to be able to tell others that you see and value what they've done for you—in the far past, or an hour ago. When I was on tour, I bought cute notecards that say "My wish for you is . . ."—and then you fill in the blank. I've sent them to a family member having a hard time (". . . to feel better"), when I'm on the outs with a friend (". . . that we can resolve our differences soon"), and *especially* when I'm feeling grateful (". . . to know how much you've helped me"). I think it's always important to let the people around you know how much they mean to you and how good they make you feel. When you initially lost your loved one, you felt numb, like you didn't want to live anymore, like you lost your best friend and probably part of your soul. So to be able to write a note that conveys gratitude toward another person? That's so huge—and, you guessed it, yet another reason to feel grateful!

Here's What Happens When You Don't Duck from Grief

One of the most incredible grief-to-gratitude stories I've had the privilege of channeling is that of Rhonda and Randy Burch, whose son Steve died at the age of twenty-three—he was hit by a subway train, but to this day his family believes it wasn't an accident. Every day, for the first three years after Steve passed, Rhonda would come home from her job at the courthouse and do her best to invoke Mariska Hargitay from *Law & Order: SVU*. She'd study Steve's hospital records and autopsy, then pore over online criminal databases to try to piece together her son's mysterious passing. Meanwhile, Rhonda's husband, Randy, threw himself into studying how subway trains worked and driving a racecar on weekends to relieve stress. Though the two were once very social, they rarely went out anymore, yet they couldn't talk about how they felt about their son's passing. Their marriage suffered as their grief unfolded at different paces and in countless ways. When Steve died, his family began to slowly die too.

For years, Rhonda felt almost assaulted by the truth that her son was no longer physically with her—a reality she wasn't at peace with. She cringed every time a friend told her Steve was "in a better place" or "You should be over it by now." Other parents cried when they saw Rhonda, or wouldn't know what to say, which made her feel forced to put on a happy face so *they'd* feel OK. To get by in private, Rhonda pretended Steve was at college. "I could not fathom to think any differently," she said. "It would physically make me sick to my stomach, and I'd ask God to take me too." As a result, Rhonda rarely slept and spent her days walking around in a fog of despair, avoiding most people who reached out to her.

After channeling Steve for his family, Rhonda and Randy felt assured that their son's spirit was safe, at peace, and still present in their lives—and this kicked off their next, healing steps both together and on their own. The couple went to grief counseling, where Rhonda finally realized, "I had to take life one minute at a time, then one hour, and then one week to get through. I learned that it's OK to be deeply, deeply sad and miss my child. We hurt deeply because we love deeply." Rhonda also gave herself a crash course in spirituality and the afterlife! She spent a lot of time reading spiritual self-help books and thinking about her purpose on earth. She ultimately resolved that life is too short to slog through it any longer. "We are only here for a little while. Recognizing what a tremendous legacy my son left and how many people's lives he's touched inspired me to want to leave a legacy like that too," she said. "I embrace the fact that I am still here because I obviously have stuff still to do on earth or I would be gone too."

As Rhonda approached acceptance that she'd never physically see her son again, she simultaneously welcomed the fact that his soul can coexist with hers on this plane. "He'll never give me a hug or call to say 'Hey, Mom, I love ya!' but his energy is everywhere," she said. "I have realized that if I keep my heart and eyes open, there is so much to see! I get signs from Steve all the time." Beyond her grief, Rhonda continues to find herself increasingly able to laugh, feel present, and surround herself with peace and positivity as much as she can. "I don't have patience for drama," she said. "I enjoy the people around me—Steve was very good at that—and try to help anyone I can, especially if they are grieving. When I know someone has lost a loved one, or a loved one is getting ready to pass, I try to always lend an ear and talk to them now, whereas before I would have stayed as far away from that subject as I could."

In the last few years, the inspiring evolution of Rhonda and Randy's growth and soul-searching has culminated in a new business that gives them purpose and calm. It manages to honor their son, strengthen their marriage, and speak to an interest that makes them happy. What makes this so amazing to me is that Rhonda and Randy didn't feel compelled to plant a garden or launch an organization related to Steve's passing in order to honor him—which would be terrific, but not them. Instead, they realized that what their souls needed to heal was a company that motivated them to live each day with gusto. So now Randy runs a private shop that sells their products, and after working a full day at the courthouse, Rhonda joins him. They travel all over the world together, and their line was recently honored in London. Steve's contribution comes in as the company's mascot—a sketch of a duck that he drew while he was alive. "That duck is seen all over the world, which is so fitting because Steve loved to travel and it keeps his memory alive," Rhonda said. "We put our love for our son into the passion we have for this company."

Gratitude plays an enormous role in Rhonda's new normal too—it keeps her spirits up, reminds her to feel positive about the future, and helps her stay focused on her work and why she does it. "Every morning when I wake up, I name five things I'm grateful for, and I do the same before bed," she told me. "If I'm really missing

Steve and having the worst day, I say five more things I'm grateful for. And then I say five things I'm grateful that he taught me about myself or my life. It might sound excessive, but it really turns things around!" How much do you love that activity? And while gratitude keeps Rhonda chugging, she knows it can't take the place of her son. "Don't get me wrong, I ache for Steve every single day," she said. "My heart never stops missing his laughter, silliness, hugs, and his voice. I have hard days. But I don't stay in my house locked away from the world and ignore every phone call anymore. I am grateful for each day that I have here. I am grateful for the little things that I used to take for granted."

View from the Top

Take a good look at your life from the top of your staircase. The view is not as terrifying as you first thought it would be, right? You're surviving. You're doing this. You are only going to get better.

Once you close this book, I'd like you to find a period of peace and quiet—on a walk, while washing dishes, wherever you can clear your head to reflect—and really think about what you've gained and learned throughout the grief process. Perhaps you've discovered resilience, self-love, forgiveness, and the ability to hear and follow your intuition and connect with Spirit in a way that you never knew possible. Because you've learned how to take care of yourself, create outlets for coping, and devise meaningful ways to celebrate and honor departed loved ones, you are now able to use these tools anytime you're feeling down, not just for grief-related reasons. I'm also certain you have a more intimate understanding of your soul, and of others' pain, which fuels compassion and acceptance. Perhaps your belief system has shifted or evolved and you've come to know God and the afterlife in a new way. I won't go so far as to call any of these aha moments a gift, but they are meaningful layers that enrich your being that didn't exist before. If you can embrace this new complexity, you will see there's a lot to appreciate.

Finally, I want you to know how grateful I am that you've allowed me to take this journey with you. When I channel your loved ones, I'm made to feel your pain as part of my job—and knowing the depths of your profound grief makes me feel so humble that you've allowed me into your soul this way. My greatest hope is that you continue to learn, grow, and honor all your life experiences, both happy and sad. And that you view every moment as a choice to live, love, honor, and respect the path of your soul.

Acknowledgments

There ain't nothing easy about working with grief, day in and day out, and I know I couldn't do it without the support and inspiration of my loved ones both here and in Heaven. It's because of your encouragement that I can do this job with a positive and grounded approach, plus an attitude of gratitude.

To my amazing coauthor, Kristina Grish, who is able to translate Spirit's words and my point of view into a book that will change readers' lives. This was the most emotionally heavy one yet, and you pulled it off with humor, heart, and perspective. And to my editor, Johanna Castillo, and publisher, Judith Curr, for continuing to champion my career as an author. I'm so grateful for the continued opportunity to share Spirit's messages that bring hope, love, and healing to the world.

To my manager, Courtney Mullin, who knew from the moment she experienced my gift that everyone else must too. And for having the utmost respect for my gift and for Spirit, and for having the faith and vision to push me past my limits in the best way—without that, none of this would be possible.

To Jonathan Partridge, who is always looking out for me with his keen input and unwavering loyalty. Thank you for being such a consistent cheerleader.

To my assistant Chris "Pergo" Pergolizzi, who's the best hipster decoy any TV celebrity could want. Thank you for stepping out of your comfort zone to work with me and for teaching me to just chill. You've embraced my world of workouts and Louboutins with open arms, and for *that*, I am grateful!

To Victoria Woods, whose social media and fan club expertise is just as impressive as her loyal friendship. Thank you for being one of my most vocal supporters and taking this journey with me.

To Magilla Entertainment and TLC, for your commitment to Spirit and the opportunity to change millions of lives every Sunday while never trying to change *me*. Your dedication is just incredible. And to my terrific crew, who are like family to me. I am so blessed to have you in my corner.

I also want to thank Rich Super from Super Artists, who "hunted me down like he wanted to marry me and have my five children"— and all he wanted me to do was a live show! And to Mills Entertainment, Brent Theatrical Lighting, and Mason Sound for making sure every detail of my shows sparkle. Thank you for your dedication and for helping me shine. I'm also grateful to Michele Emanuele for her elegant and generous taste, and to my attorney Jeff Cohen for being my little pit bull.

To all my friends who've stood by me, including Sandy Riccardi, Lauran Zlotolow, Eileen Baachi, and Desiree Simonelli. No matter how much time we spend together, our friendship always means the world to me.

To Regina Murphy, for continuing to allow me to share Bryan's and Bill's legacies in my books. They are still doing God's work, even from the Other Side, and I'm so honored to be part of their story.

To my extended family on both sides, especially Aunt Debbie, for all her support, and Aunt Gina, for sharing her grief journey in such a public way. And to my sister-cousin Lisa Brigandi, who is still my go-to source for champagne and belly laughs. What would I do without you guys?

To my parents, Ronnie and Nick, for giving me the most amazing life and encouraging me to believe in myself. You've shown me love, encouragement, and what family really is about. I am a better woman, parent, wife, friend, and community member because of you. I also want to thank my brother, Michael, and his family for always insisting that no matter how busy we are, we're never too busy for each other. I'm appreciative too of my family in Spirit, including Nanny, Pop, Gram, and Gramps for guiding and protecting me. And for those who've passed since my last book, Uncle Louie and Cousin Lois, for recently joining Spirit Team Caputo! And to Connie, Jack, and the rest of the Caputos for all your prayers, even though I don't call as much as I should (I know, I know . . .).

To my husband, Larry, who is my absolute rock. There aren't many men who'd be able to unwaveringly encourage and stand by me the way you do. Thank you for being you, and for allowing me to be me. And to Larry and Victoria, who, by supporting all of my out-of-the-box decisions, have shown me how to be a better parent and to support *their* out-of-the-box choices too (companionism and beauty school come to mind).

Last but never least, I'm deeply thankful to God and Spirit, for giving me my gift and helping me channel in creative ways that allow for healing. And to my fans and clients who inspire and touch me every day with their optimism, strength, and mind-blowing stories. It is not easy to live in your skin, and I am in awe of how much you've endured and yet are able to gracefully persevere. You are the reason I get up every morning to do what I do, and I hope that I can contribute to your life as much as you do to mine.

xoxo,

Theresa